Out of Hitler's Shadow

Childhood and Youth in Germany and the United States, 1935-1967

Roderick Stackelberg

iUniverse, Inc.
New York Bloomington

Out of Hitler's Shadow
Childhood and Youth in Germany and the United States, 1935-1967

iUniverse books may be ordered through booksellers or by contacting:

iUniverse
1663 Liberty Drive
Bloomington, IN 47403
www.iuniverse.com
1-800-Authors (1-800-288-4677)

ISBN: 978-1-4502-6033-6 (pbk)
ISBN: 978-1-4502-6034-3 (cloth)
ISBN: 978-1-4502-6035-0 (ebk)

Printed in the United States of America

iUniverse rev. date: 10/5/2010

Contents

Prologue

"*The Unexamined Life is not worth living.*" Socrates

"*Life is lived forward and understood backward.*" Kierkegaard

"*We have finished with the past, but the past has not finished with us." "Das Vergessen der Vernichtung ist Teil der Vernichtung selbst:" Lebensgeschichten von Opfern der nationalsozialistischen "Euthanasie."* (Göttingen: Wallstein, 2007)

"*It's hard to write honestly about oneself.*" Blayne Kinsey, senior at Lake Region Union High School in Barton, Vermont, 1968-1969

My main reason for presuming to write an autobiography is that I have an unusual story to tell, particularly of my early years. It cannot compete, in sheer tragic force, with the many hundreds of Holocaust survival memoirs on the market. But my story is unusual enough to command some interest beyond my immediate family. Born in 1935 to an American mother and a German father, I grew up in Nazi Germany during the Second World War. My mother could trace her American background on her father's side to well before the Revolutionary war. On her mother's side she was the descendant of the Irish patriots Robert and Thomas Addis Emmet. The former was hanged by the British at the age of 25 for organizing the failed insurrection of 1803; the latter, his older brother, who was heavily involved in the aborted Uprising of 1798, was banished from Ireland. He emigrated to the United States, where he founded the American branch of the family and became the attorney general of the state of New York. Today there are more than 400 living descendants of Thomas Addis Emmet, a large number of whom gathered in Ireland for a week's celebration to commemorate the 200th anniversary of the 1798 revolt. A similar gathering took place in New York City on the 200th anniversary of Robert Emmet's trial and execution in 2003.

My father was a Baltic German aristocrat whose immediate family left their Estonian homeland for Germany in 1919 after their estate was expropriated by the newly-independent Estonian Republic. The Stackelbergs could trace their ancestry back to the thirteenth century. Stackelbergs had lived in what would become Latvia and Estonia for seven centuries before their final expulsion as a result of the Hitler-Stalin Non-Agression Pact in 1939. My father and mother met as expatriate students in Munich in 1931. Despite the basic incompatibilities that would lead to their divorce after a decade of marriage, they fell in love and produced four children together between 1932 and 1938. What they shared in common was a sense of displacement from the countries of their birth. Their German-American marriage ended in divorce in 1942 at the height of the Second World War.

The war itself is the subject of only one chapter in this memoir—Chapter 2. Yet it forms the crucial background to this volume and to my recollections as a whole. By 1967, the year in which this first volume ends, I had spent exactly half my life, sixteen years each, in Germany and the United States (if the eighteen months that I spent in Germany as a draftee in the U.S. army in 1959-1960 is counted as part of my American experience). The unanswered (and probably unanswerable) question underlying the events in this first volume, which traces my life up to age 32, is to what degree my experience of the war and Nazism in Germany as a child may account for my peculiar biography as a young man after the war. Hence my choice for what may seem like an excessively dramatic title, which also reflects my lifelong obsession with exploring the roots of National Socialism. Although I graduated from Harvard at barely age 21, I squandered several opportunities to pursue a normal career path before finally returning to graduate school at age 35. I do not offer any excuses for what from the perspective of normal professional success can only be described as a wasted youth. The trauma of war was certainly no impediment to my older brother Olaf's successful academic career. In any case, no experience is ever entirely wasted, even when it seems not to have yielded any visible benefit.

Writing my memoirs has been an interesting experience. My purpose was to leave as honest a record of how I experienced the events in my life as my self-knowledge, temperament, and talent or lack of it would permit. Like Rousseau in his *Confessions*, I set out to tell the unvarnished truth about my life. But like Rousseau, his claims to the contrary notwithstanding, I have found this to be impossible. Even if it were possible to write the full truth about oneself, that kind of memoir could only be published posthumously, if at all! The risk of giving offense and the urge to gloss over unpleasant truths (not to mention the fallibility of memory and the hazards of self-analysis) are simply too great. Paradoxically, it may be possible to be totally honest in fiction, which is not subject to the same limitations as (auto)biography and allows the author more freedom to explore the full range of human experiences, but it's too late for me to start on that ambitious genre (though some family members might think that in writing my memoirs I *am* indulging in fiction!) So I limited my ambitions. I have not revealed every one of my hidden thoughts about people or events, but I have not sought to conceal or disguise my basic opinions and beliefs, a fact that will probably become even more apparent to readers who disagree with my personal biases than to those who share them. I am continuing with this project, imperfect though it may be, because a descendant or a future generation may find in it some useful insight into their past. For some readers this first volume might also provide a window into the 1940s, 1950s, and 1960s. And some readers might even find the book entertaining in the present.

I have had the advantage of being able to refer to personal journals that I began keeping as a seven-year-old boy in Germany in 1942. I broke them off under the cultural shock of our return to the United States in 1946 and then resumed them in English as a nineteen-year-old college student in 1954. My account of the intervening years, 1946 to 1954, are perforce based more on memory and on whatever documentation may have been available from my school and early college years. My journals were never intended for anything but my personal use. I can't claim to have been entirely indifferent to what others might have thought of what I wrote, but eventual posthumous (or clandestine) readers were never my target audience or my main concern. At some point in old age I drew the logical conclusion: when there is not enough time left to reread my journals, it's time to stop writing them. My journals have grown significantly shorter over the years, especially after I started on the present project.

Many details of fact and chronology also have been checked with my older brother Olaf, my sister Betsy, and my younger brother Tempy, each of whom made contributions of some kind to this memoir. I owe a special debt to Olaf, who cooperated in the task of recalling our childhood and youth by sharing with me his particular perspective. We did not always agree—and I'm sure there is still much he would disapprove of—but his contributions were invaluable and his openness and willingness to offer constructive criticism is much appreciated. My greatest debt is to my wife Sally and our son Emmet, without whose support and encouragement I would probably never even have started this book, let alone completed it.

1
Mama and Papa: The 1930s

One of my great regrets is that I never asked Mama to tell her story of how, or even exactly when, she came to Germany, fell in love with my father, and decided to stay for what would turn out to be more than fifteen years, including the entire Second World War. The bare outlines of her life are discernible and easy to trace, but unfortunately I know few of the details and little of her inner life. This is what I know: My mother Ellen (1912-1998) was born in New York on 20 January 1912 as the youngest and somewhat pampered daughter of Nicholas Biddle (1878-1923), a wealthy financier who managed the estate of John Jacob Astor (1864-1912) after the latter's death on the Titanic. Ellen's mother was Elisabeth Le Roy Emmet (1874-1943), member of a socially prominent Irish-American family and direct descendant of Thomas Addis Emmet (1764-1827), who was forced to flee to America after the execution of his brother, the Irish patriot Robert Emmet (1778-1803).

Granny Elisabeth Emmet Biddle

Grandfather Nicholas Biddle

Ellen was not an easy child. She was strong-willed and adventurous, imaginative (according to her first cousin and playmate, 'Sis' Lapsley [1913-1993]) and rebellious. Ellen was dismissed from the prestigious Miss Chapin's School for girls in the late 1920s for insubordination, although I never did find out the specific act for which she was thrown out. It was not on academic grounds. Thereupon her mother decided to take her to Europe on a 'grand tour.' In the summer of 1930 Ellen and her mother, along with several other members of the Emmet family, stayed as paying guests at Schloß Neubeuern in the Bavarian Alps, the ancestral Wendelstadt family castle then owned by Baroness Julie "Sisi" von Wendelstadt (1871-1942) after the death of her husband Jan von Wendelstadt (1855-1909). Here and at 'Hinterhör,' the modest farm estate in neighboring Altenbeuern deeded by Jan Wendelstadt to Sisi's sister-in-law (Sisi's brother's widow) Countess Ottonie 'Sweety' von Degenfeld-Schonburg (1882-1970), Ellen met my father, Baron Curt Ernst Ferdinand Friedrich von Stackelberg (1910-1994), an impoverished Baltic German student at the University of Munich who was earning some of his expenses as a tennis coach to the guests at Hinterhör and to the students at Schloss Neubeuern (which housed a boys' private school founded by Sisi Wendelstadt and Sweety Degenfeld in 1925). The wealthy American and impoverished aristocrat fell passionately in love. Ellen decided to remain in Munich to study art, apparently over her mother's objections. Granny did not think highly of my father and thought him unsuitable for Mama. Undeterred, Mama got pregnant and they married rather abruptly on New Year's Eve 1931. My older brother Olaf Patrik, named after his paternal grandfather, was born in Munich on 2 August 1932, ending Mama's career in art before it got properly started.

Mama and Papa, 1932

While Germany underwent the exuberant turmoil of a 'national revolution' after Hitler's sudden appointment to the chancellorship at the end of January 1933, Papa continued to study law in Munich, now financially supported by his American mother-in-law, our Granny, while Mama stayed home with her growing family. My sister Betsy (named after her maternal grandmother) was born on 27 April 1934 and my birth followed, rather unexpectedly, on 8 May 1935. Mama, who had been nursing Betsy when I was conceived, did not discover her pregnancy until three months before my birth. It was a difficult birth, and she and I spent my first three months in the hospital. Her marriage was already beginning to go sour before Papa moved his family to Berlin in September 1936 to complete the year of in-service training required for a career in law. My younger brother Nicholas Temple was born in Berlin on 23 December 1938. This was one of my earliest memories, indelibly imprinted in my mind because of the scratch I received from the brooch Mama was wearing when she came back from the hospital. Years later Fritzi von Kügelgen, a close friend of the family, referred to Tempy as the prospective *Versöhnungskind* on whom rested his parents' hopes of reconciling a marriage that was falling apart.

Ellen and Curt had very different personalities; in retrospect their relationship seems to prove nothing so much as that 'opposites attract.' While Mama was by nature independent, non-conformist, a dare-devil and a risk-taker, always ready and willing to defy convention and leave the beaten track, Papa was socially and professionally ambitious, much more cautious and correct than Mama, at least in his public conduct, and very aware of the obligations he thought he owed to his background as the descendant of an ancient Baltic aristocratic family. The emblematic story of their thorny relationship was that Papa had been unable to dissuade Mama from attending an aristocratic ball in her ski-boots. But Mama made merciless fun of Papa doffing his hat in obeisance to his unseen interlocutor as he deferentially answered the phone. Many years later, unconscious of the irony in his idealization of a normal middle-class lifestyle, Papa told me in an apologetic tone, '*Mit deiner Mutter war kein bürgerliches Leben zu führen*' (with your mother a bourgeois life was not possible). However, he prized a visible dent she had once put in his desk in a fit of jealousy, provoked, it seems, more by his addiction to work than by any actual infidelity, although, according to Mama, there was some of that encumbering their marriage as well.

Mama and Papa at Hinterhör

Mama with Olaf, 1933

Each of us children bore some marks of our conflicting maternal and paternal heritages. In retrospect Olaf and Betsy took more after Papa, both in physical appearance and in other ways, and Tempy and I took more after Mama. Olaf became the "*Aushängeschild der Familie*" (the quote is again from Fritzi, meaning, roughly, "poster child"), professionally the most successful of the four of us, eventually ending his career as head of the Mathematics Department at Kent State University for twenty years.

Olaf at Hinterhör, 1936

Betsy and Mama were always at odds, just as different from each other in their tastes, opinions, values, and personalities as were Papa amd Mama. Mama herself always thought that Tempy was most like her, irreverent, insouciant, irascible and independent, and both shared a particularly cutting brand of humor. As for myself, I have always been conscious of my conflicted identity and divided loyalties. I admired Papa (after I got to know him in 1959), but have always felt much closer to and more like Mama. Looking back over my life, I am struck by how much I replicated some aspects of her peculiar biography: becoming an expatriate in my twenties, spurning a normal academic career path, marrying and then divorcing a German, never fulfilling my own literary or artistic ambitions, living my life at the edge of poverty (at least until finally securing a permanent job at the age of 43), though never as badly off as Mama after the war. Mama, however, thrived on activity, whether it had a purposeful goal or not. "That ability to sit at your desk for hours," she told me when I was working on a paper for college, "that's something you have from your father, not from me."

Betsy, Tempy, and Rodi, 1940

Papa's youth had not been easy. His Stackelberg ancestors, whose line he could trace back to the thirteenth century, had migrated east as part of the Teutonic Order, and settled in the Baltic provinces of Livland, Kurland, and Estland (today Latvia and Estonia) as part of the culturally German land-owning ruling class. Formerly subject to the kingdom of Sweden (there are still sizable branches of the Stackelberg family in both Sweden and Finland), the Baltic provinces had been incorporated into the Russian Empire under Peter the Great in the Great Northern War of the early eighteenth century. Papa was born in the imperial capital of St. Petersburg on 12 May 1910 by the old Julian calendar still in use in Russia at the time.

Opa, Oma, and Papa, St. Petersburg, 1910

During the First World War, most of the Baltic aristocracy remained loyal to the Russian monarchy and fought on the Russean side. After the fall of the tsar and the violent Bolshevik Revolution that followed, Estonia and Latvia declared their independence from Russia as self-governing democratic republics. Latvia and parts of Estonia were occupied by German troops until 1919, when they were withdrawn under the terms of the Treaty of Versailles, signed in June 1919. It was then that the fledgling Estonian government was able to push through the expropriation of baronial estates. The Baltic-German aristocracy lost its political dominance as well as much of its land. Among the properties confiscated by the new Estonian state was Hallinap, the estate managed by Papa's father Olaf Patrik (1878-1959) on behalf of the Stackelberg Family Foundation, incorporated under Russian Imperial law in 1864 to assist indigent members of the large Stackelberg Family clan.

Opa with Papa at Hallinap, 1912

Faced with the loss of their livelihood, Papa's father and mother, born Stella Bernewitz (1883-1950), emigrated to Germany with their two children, my nine-year-old father and his seven-year-old sister Elisabeth ("Lulli"). Papa's aged paternal grandparents remained on their reduced family estate of Röal, where they died in their eighties in 1925.

Life in Germany was difficult for our father's transplanted family in the aftermath of the First World War. Deprived of their legal privileges in the new Weimar republic, many members of the lower aristocracy found it difficult to maintain, or in the case of the displaced Baltic aristocracy to regain, the status and standard of living to which they had been accustomed. Adjustment to very different conditions and regret for the loss of their inherited way of life in their ancient homeland must certainly have left some psychic scars. Papa's parents finally found reasonably suitable employment as the managers of a rest-home for convalescents in the alpine health resort town of Bad Reichenhall in Bavaria.

Papa's mother, aunt (at the piano), and grandparents at Röal, 1912

Papa's youth was marked by the kind of genteel poverty that may well have led him to value money and status so greatly later in life—another trait that would differentiate him from my mother, although, ironically, she grew up under much wealthier circumstances. Ellen's silk-stocking, social-register American background dated back on the Biddle side to well before the American Revolution, in which one of our Biddle ancestors served as the Qartermaster-General of George Washington's army and another young Biddle, a naval officer, was killed. Mama's background must have seemed as exotic and attractive to Curt as his own aristocratic pedigree probably did to her.

Papa at age fifteen, 1925

It is tempting to see the breakdown of their cosmopolitan marriage as also a German-American conflict in which the personal and the political inevitably overlapped. The war put their marriage to a terrible test and clarified for Mama once and for all where her loyalties lay. In retrospect it does not seem a mere coincidence that their formal break-up occurred in the year that the United States and Germany went to war against each other. Their divorce did not become final until June 1942. By that time Curt had fathered a daughter, Susanne (b. April 1942), with an attractive blond Polish woman, Halina Wojciechova (1913-2001) from Cracow. He was stationed in Poland as an officer in the Quartermaster Corps of the Wehrmacht, into which he had been conscripted in 1940. In his memoirs, written in the 1980s, Papa wrote that before pursuing his courtship of Halina he had offered to continue his marriage with Mama, but Mama had rejected his efforts at reconciliation. Mama corroborated his account, but with the significant difference that when he made his offer of reconciliation Halina was already expecting his child. After obtaining the official permission required for an "interracial" marriage, Papa married his second wife in November 1942, and they had two more daughters, Stella (b. 1943) and Sylvia (b. 1945). The last of his eight children, his son Curt Jr. (1956-1997), was born eleven years later in Karlsruhe.

Betsy, Tempy, Olaf, and Rodi in Berlin, 1939

Years later I asked Mama why she had chosen to remain in Germany despite her dislike of the Nazis, their vicious persecution of Germany's Jewish minority, their contempt for American popular culture and humanitarian values, and the absence of any of the democratic freedoms with which she had grown up. She experienced her first visit to pre-Hitler Germany as a 'culture shock,' but an exciting one with both positive and negative features. As is often the case with young people, she was politically aloof without strong ideological convictions, although a partisan supporter of Roosevelt's New Deal at home. From Papa's relatively more conservative perspective she had left-wing sympathies, which certainly came to the fore under very different circumstances upon her return to the United States after the war. Once married in Germany she evidently saw no compelling reason to leave the country to which her husband was bound by both ancestral lineage and the prospects of future professional success. Mama did once confess to me that she would not have wanted to stay in Germany if she had not married into the aristocracy. The deference she enjoyed as *'Frau Baronin'* in a class-conscious society was certainly one of the perks that came with her marriage to a German aristocrat. It was not as if she had no opportunity to leave. With her children (but without Papa, whose work kept him busy) she made several lengthy visits back to her mother's seaside summer home in Wareham, Massachusetts, in the 1930s: once in 1934 to show off her latest child Betsy, again in 1937, and finally in the summer of 1939, along with our German maid, Fräulein Ursula ('Ulla') Fuchs.

Wareham, 1937. Back row: Mama, Granny, and Aunt Virginia with Liz; middle row: Olaf, Ginny, Kitty, and Shuby (dog); front row: Betsy and Rodi

By the time Mama returned to Europe in September 1939, three weeks after she had originally intended to return, the German invasion of Poland had already begun. Why did she decide to return to a troubled marriage in a Germany at war when she certainly could have stayed in safe and comfortable circumstances surrounded by a supportive family in the country of her birth? Of course, nobody knew at the time that the German invasion of Poland marked the beginning of what was to become a second world war. The likelihood of the United States becoming involved in the war, if it was not attacked, seemed quite remote at the time. For Mama the reason she returned to Germany was self-evident: her place, she said, was beside her husband, even, or especially, in time of war. But in view of the continuing problems in her marriage, this uncharacteristically conventional explanation did not ring entirely true. Papa's explanation was predictably less charitable, reflecting the bitterness of their divorce: she had formed a strong attachment to the talented Dutch music student Winifred ('Wini') Van Duyl (1913-2007), whom she had met in Berlin and wanted to rejoin. Besides, he added, but with a hint of embarrassment at so outrageous a suggestion, she wanted to be on the winning side. My brother Olaf attributed Mama's decision to return to Germany to her wish to escape from the domination of her mother and older sister. Family pressure to get her to stay in America only made her want to return all the more. My first wife Steffi Heuss (b. 1941), who did not get along with her mother-in-law, but was a perceptive critic, had a provocative explanation of her own: 'Can you really imagine Mama missing out on the war?"

2
The War: 1939-1945

The start of the war forced us to return to Europe via still neutral Italy where Papa met us in Trieste and we returned to Berlin by train. On the way I caused some embarrassment by loudly inquiring in English, 'Are we in Germany yet?' We were instructed no longer to speak English in public. Our ship, the Saturnia, had been briefly detained in Gibraltar to unload the cargo of copper that it had been carrying. My clearest early childhood memories are of this trip, or more specifically, of the preparations for it. I clearly remember my fright at being told that I would have to jump from the boarding plank onto the ship or else I would fall into the sea. Papa claimed that Mama had a sadistic streak—she certainly took to German-style corporal punishment rather too readily—but more fundamentally she believed in teasing as a pedagogical and disciplinary method. Foibles and conceits should be driven out of children by poking merciless fun. The most contemptible vices in her eyes were cowardice, servility, dishonesty, and selfishness. She had no tolerance at all for timidity, even in children, especially her own. I was a 'Tolpatsch,' a physically clumsy child and notoriously risk-averse in a culture that prized physical courage (and ability) above all. Mama finally lost patience with my inability to swim (Betsy had famously learned as early as age four), so when I turned nine in 1944 but still could not swim she simply threw me into the deep end of the local public swimming pool in Ried, the Bavarian village where we then lived. Of course she would not have let me drown, but I was not at all convinced that she wouldn't at the time. I swallowed quite a bit of water, but I did learn, although it took considerably longer for me to ratchet up enough courage to learn how to dive as well.

Mama was strict and severe with us children, as was customary in Germany at the time. In school we received *Tatzen*, lashes on the palm of the hand, for misbehavior or errors, the most painful effect of which was the humiliation of being punished in front of the class. Even small misdemeanors at home could result in a spanking with the wooden clothes hangers Mama preferred for this purpose. "If you're going to cry," she would say before administering punishment, "I'll give you something to cry about." A memorable outburst of rage occurred on the day she returned from Munich after the finalization of her divorce in summer 1942. It was one of the few times I can remember that Wini, who usually kept out of these punitive rituals, intervened on our behalf and told Mama that she was going too far. The benign effect of Mama's all-too-foreseeable *schimpfings* was to strengthen an underground solidarity among us children, to the point where we even invented secret languages, jokes, and games that none of the adults could share. Although it would be hard for me to explain today just how and why these secret understandings with my siblings cast such a magic spell on my childhood, I later felt grateful to Mama for bringing us children so closely together, much closer than we ever became when we were grown. Although Betsy, who along with Olaf bore the brunt of Mama's wrath, would probably disagree, I often thought that Mama's harsh upbringing had done us a favor. It didn't generate self-confidence (or self-esteem in today's jargon), but it paradoxically eased our path in the world by making us liked and admired for our good manners and disciplined behavior.

The war did not really come home to us, or at least not to me, until the summer of 1940 after the fall of France. Before then the main effect of the war on my life was the punishment meted out to us children for careless infractions of the nightly blackouts and the fact that we could no longer get chocolate at the candy store (rationing had begun on the day the war started). I do distinctly remember viewing the great victory parade in Berlin from the window of Papa's law firm on Unter den Linden, the grand tree-lined boulevard that led through the heart of the city from the Brandenburg Gate in the west to the Alexanderplatz in the east. After vacationing in Hinterhör in the summer of 1940, as we had often done in the past, we returned to Berlin in the fall of 1940. Now, at the height of the London Blitz, Berlin was beginning to experience the first retaliatory bombing attacks. Mama kept a journal for each of us children, in which she sporadically recorded our activities and reactions, especially when there was something comical about them. One night, when the anti-aircraft fire of the Flak was particularly intense, I told her in the peculiar mixture of English and German that we children used, 'Rodi is not afraid that the Engländer will come too next the Gardinen.' I did concede, however, that 'My heart klopps a little rascher, Mama.' Refractory as ever, Mama refused to go down to the cellar that served as the air-raid shelter, but by winter 1940-1941 she did send us children down with Ulla (refusal to seek shelter was officially regarded as sabotaging the war effort). Papa had already been drafted and was no longer at home. One of my clearest memories is of the musty smell, not unpleasant, but unmistakably below ground level, as we wrapped ourselves in blankets on benches and waited for the *Entwarnung* (all-clear) sirens to sound. I also remember gawking at the roped-off section of the street not far from our apartment house where you could look through a bomb crater right down onto the Ubahn tracks.

Everything changed in 1941. Papa was now in the war, as most young men were, and in the spring we moved to rural southern Bavaria, some 40 miles south of Munich, to get away from the bombing in Berlin. The tiny peasant village of Ried bei Benediktbeuern, today Kreis Kochel, was to be our home for the next three-and-a-half years. Life was surprisingly stable and peaceful here, at least for us children, until 1944. When I think of life in Germany during the war I associate it mainly with Ried. Dairy farming was the only economically productive activity in Ried. The characteristic sound in this hamlet was that of cowbells, alerting farmers to the whereabouts of their herds. The characteristic smell was that of manure, emanating from the many open piles in the neighborhood. Farming was labor-intensive and un-mechanized. Teams of oxen were used to plough the fields and haul the fresh grass or the hay to feed the herds. Better-off farmers may have owned horses before the war, but they had all been requisitioned by now. I never saw a tractor at any time during the war. The grass was cut by hand with scythes or sickles, raked by hand, and lifted onto the wooden oxcarts with pitchforks. Women did much of the work. All milking was done by hand, as it had been for centuries. In Benediktbeuern I began school as a six-year-old in September 1941. We walked one-and-a-half miles to school at the Bendiktine monastery every day, where we also attended mass every Sunday. Mama later said that she had hoped that the Church would offer us children a stand-in for our absent father. I remember despairing that I would never have the strength of renunciation required to become a Catholic priest. The injunction against touching one's private parts was among the hardest to meet.

Mama with Stevie in Ried, 1941

From a childhood perspective life in parochial Bavaria was entirely normal as we had no other norm to compare it to. We vaguely knew that Ried was only our temporary home, but we had no idea what would follow. We took regular piano lessons, played concerts on the recorder, learned poems by heart, put on puppet shows (usually historical dramas on the military exploits of such heroic figures as Charlemagne and Otto the Great), and were tutored in Latin, geography, and *Naturkunde* ('nature studies') on the side. I knew there was a war on, a terrible struggle for national existence, but that seemed to be normal, too. Peace was an unreal, utopian state of affairs that might come once every few decades or so. I had no sense of Germany as the aggressor in the war. Enemies were, after all, all around us. Didn't Germany have to fight off the whole world from 1914 to 1918? I simply assumed that Germany was forced to defend itself against intractable foes. That is what we were told in school, always with a scornful reference to the injustice 'we' suffered when the world ganged up on 'us' in the *Weltkrieg*. From a child's point of view it seemed natural to root for the home team. It came as quite a shock when Mama told me, late in the war (when she thought I was old enough to be trusted) that Hitler was 'insane.' In school we were given names of young German soldiers on the eastern front to whom we were urged to write letters of support and encouragement to keep up their spirits. I did so, probably in 1942, and received a remarkably warm and grateful response from my pen pal deep in the heart of Russia. I remember the sense of guilt I felt for not answering that letter (or maybe a later one). I stopped writing back not for any principled reason, but because of growing disinterest and not knowing what to say under obviously deteriorating circumstances. By that time the war was going badly, as even we children couldn't help but realize. In the later years of the war we were often bullied by schoolmates and mocked as 'Amis' on our increasingly scary walks home from school. Even our neighbor and long-time playmate Hansi Neuner turned against us (or refused to speak up for us) when he was with his buddies from school.

Lunch in the back yard in Ried, 1941 (with Ulla, right, and Wini, behind Mama)

Olaf had somewhat different memories than I did. At no time, he tells me, did he "root for the home team" or hope that Germany would win the war "One thing that emerges quickly," he wrote me after reading my account, "is that we saw things in different ways, not unsurprisingly. I cannot remember ever feeling 'at home' in Germany, from our days in Ried onward, nor in the latter days of our Berlin stay. This feeling has never completely gone away, from St. Paul's days to wherever I've lived, and I may have inherited that feeling of homelessness from Papa. I remember you being enthusiastic about our great army victories, meaning the German army, presenting plays for us in Ried, written and organized by you, and Betsy remembers being 'a little Nazi.' Mama told me that in a year or two you would be backing the Allied armies; we should not interrupt your creativity. I was of course significantly older. From my earliest memories (being chased by neighborhood boys in Berlin returning from an errand Mama had sent me on, to buy milk, I think it was) I always felt an outsider in German surroundings. I had an instinctive fear of and aversion to the Nazi political scene, no doubt instilled by Mama. I do remember the caution she advised us to take in speaking to others outside the family. You were barely nine and I was pushing twelve at the time of the Normandy invasion, and by then I think you were back into reality, as I recall. I remember Mama giving us briefings about the invasion in our room in the *Tenne* (attic) after dark."

Tempy with Toni Neuner (left) in Ried, 1941

In the early and middle stages of the war, its most noticeable effect on us children was the shortage of food, although in the countryside we were certainly better off than we would have been in the city. In 1942 and 1943 every available square foot of our yard was converted into a vegetable garden, overseen by Wini, who spent the entire war with us in our retrospectively quite idyllic Bavarian refuge. I remember her Dutch brother Ronald, who had joined the SS, being pressed into duty turning over the soil by hand, a chore he performed with obvious reluctance on one of his infrequent visits to Ried. Our diet consisted mainly of potatoes, which we ate for breakfast, lunch, and supper. But we had plenty of vegetables during the summer and fall. One day every spring we would get up very early to fetch our allotment of tomato seedlings, a certain fixed number per person, distributed to local residents at the monastery in Benediktbeuern. Because we had no refrigeration, our meager ration of milk was allowed to turn sour in soup plates on window sills until it turned solid and had to be eaten with a spoon. It always made me sick, but I was forced to eat, even if I vomited it all back up. We did have meat early in the war—our local *Wirtshaus*, Lauterbacher's, had a small slaughterhouse in back, where I witnessed the terrified howls of animals strung up by their hind legs to be killed.

Betsy and Olaf in a rowboat on the Kochelsee during the war

Later in the war, when meat was hard to come by, Mama was forced to improvise. When later she was asked how she had managed to feed her family during the war, she said, 'I hope I never have to eat another woodchuck in my life.' She was very inventive, however, in turning almost every organic product into some sort of soup. Only rarely, as far as I can remember, her *Sandsuppe,* as we called it, turned out to be totally inedible and had to be thrown out. We children stole fruit from trees in the neighborhood whenever we could, although it was strictly *verboten*. An apple or a pear was our greatest luxury. We children were also enlisted in all-day family expeditions into the alpine foothills to gather wild strawberries, raspberries, and blackberries at different stages of the summer. But *naschen* was strictly forbidden, lest there not be enough to bring home. We were also sent out to scrounge for wood in the forests, especially when coal grew very scarce. Ultimately we heated only a single room, in which Mama, Betsy, and Tempy also slept. Wini had an unheated room of her own next door. We did all our cooking on our pot-bellied stove and made our own soap with scraps of fat and the rations of glycerine that were made available to the public for that purpose. The kitchen was never used in the winter. Olaf and I slept in the bitterly cold *Eiskeller* in the *Tenne* above the former stable, the back part of the house that had been used to store grain and hay.

We children had all the 'childhood illnesses,' except diphtheria, which loomed as the most dreaded disease, from which, at periodic intervals, one or another of our schoolmates died. We three older children had scarlet fever together, in early 1942, and lay in the same well-heated room for eight weeks, a time we remembered as one of the coziest periods of our childhood. In the spring of 1942 I was diagnosed with tuberculosis and missed three months of school. Mama schooled me at home, and I remember deliberately making mistakes to test the accuracy of her corrections! After returning to school in the fall of 1942 I had to lie outdoors for three hours a day (the so-called *Liegekur*) until I was pronounced cured in the spring of 1943. Betsy, too, who suffered from asthma, missed a lot of school. Later in the war the number of residents in our house expanded to accommodate additional evacuees from Berlin. The family that moved in with us were the Massenbachs. Clare von Massenbach was an English woman who, like Mama, had married a German baron now conscripted into the war. Her sons Peter and Hans-Christoph were roughly the ages of Betsy and Tempy, respectively. Clare had already known Mama in Berlin, and their husbands were also good friends. Clare was deeply religious. I remember passing her bedroom one night and seeing her kneeling by her bedside deep in prayer. I was told that Clare never quite got over the loss of her husband, who was killed in the last days of the war. She returned to England at the end of 1945, establishing a new home for her sons and providing for their education. Her son Hans-Christoph would go on to a career of over thirty years in the British Foreign Office, mostly engaged in Anglo-German trade promotion.

Clare von Massenbach and her sons Peter and Hans-Christoph

In November 1942 Sisi Wendelstadt, Betsy's godmother, died in Neubeuern shortly before she would have had to vacate her *Schloß,* which had been expropriated by the Nazi government earlier that year. The private school for boys she and Sweety had established on the grounds of the *Schloß* in 1925 had been closed and converted into a NAPOLA school for the training and indoctrination of party leaders. Mama, Betsy, and I traveled from Ried to attend Sisi's funeral, an event that left a lasting impression in my mind, bringing home to me, as nothing had before, the impermanence of life, even its most venerable institutions. Sisi's funeral procession stretched the entire two kilometers separating the village of Neubeuern from the family mausoleum in neighboring Altenbeuern. After the war Sweety succeeded in refounding the school under its former director. It remains in operation to this day.

Mama's and Wini's closest friends in Ried were Maria Marc (1887-1955), the widow of the expressionist painter Franz Marc (1880-1916), killed in the First World War, and the Polish-Jewish composer Heinrich Kaminski (1886-1946), who shared Frau Marc's large house and used a shed in her yard as his studio. Wini studied music and played the violin with him. Mama and Wini exchanged frequent visits with Frau Marc and Professor Kaminski (as he was known to us children). Despite his Jewish background, Kaminski survived the war, thanks, no doubt in part to the fact that Ried lay off the beaten path. According to Mama, he was protected by a local official who insisted that Kaminski wasn't Jewish, but merely a German 'of the Mosaic faith'! Kaminski also benefited from his status of a Jew in a mixed marriage and the father of *Mischlinge.* He had been married to an ethnically German woman, with whom he had raised three children, two of whom were killed in the war, one of them in combat in the Wehrmacht. We children marveled at Kaminski's concentrated and implicitly defiant way of walking, oblivious to the people around him, his eyes always fixed on the distant horizon straight ahead. He was also much in demand for his knowledge of homeopathic remedies. I remember how we prized Arnica, a plant found in the alpine foothills around Ried, as the best means of warding off infections when applied to open wounds or injuries. Other members of Ried's little circle of clandestine dissidents, most, like Frau Marc and Kaminski, a generation older than Mama and Wini, were the displaced aristocrats Frau Dorothee von Velsen (a leading proponent of women's rights) and Herr and Frau von Delius (to whom we children went for our weekly lessons in *Naturkunde*). Although strongly anti-Nazi, they were much more pessimistic than Mama at least until 1943: they were sure that nothing could stop the Nazis from winning the war. With typically American optimism Mama was the only one who never doubted that Germany would ultimately lose. After the war Marc, Kaminiski, and von Velsen all had streets named after them in Ried.

Papa on a visit to Ried, 1942

In 1944 the war came much closer to home. Early that year Mama received a letter from Miss Mary Foote (1872-1968), an old family friend, a celebrated former artist, and now personal secretary to Carl Jung (1865-1961) in Zurich, that Mama's mother had collapsed and died of a heart attack in her New York City apartment at the age of 69. Betsy later recalled that this was the first of only two times in her life that she had ever seen Mama cry (the second time was early in the morning of 15 July 1946, when we passed by the Statue of Liberty in the entrance to New York Harbor on our return to the United States). Granny had been on her way to her sister in Bedford, Aunt Eleanor Emmet Lapsley (1880-1953), who had just learned the sad news that her younger son David (1919-1944) had been killed on an Air Corps training flight. Her older son Howdy (1910-1942) had been killed in a similar training accident two years earlier. By the summer of 1944 the signs that Germany had lost the war were unmistakable. We children counted the huge armadas of 'flying fortresses' that flew at great height in perfect formations from their bases in Italy on their way to Munich, unimpeded by German fighters or Flak. A few minutes after they passed overhead we heard the characteristic whining sound of falling bombs and then the massive explosions as they dropped their lethal cargoes on the city. On our summer excursions to the nearby Loisach River to swim, we picked up leaflets dropped from the skies exhorting Germans to turn against their government and threatening utter destruction if they failed to do so. We also picked up the metal strips the bombers dropped, apparently to confuse the accuracy of the Flak. Yet the war went on: convoys of Wehrmacht trucks carried supplies south to the Italian front on the *Landstrasse* that passed in front of our house. Small detachments of replacement troops even trained for combat in Ried, scurrying with rifles at the ready from one covered position to another to the staccato barks of their sergeants. It must have been that summer, too, that I overheard Mama say that all Jews were being killed. She had heard that improbable report not from any official German source, but from the French and Polish prisoners of war assigned as forced laborers to peasant farmsteads in Ried. 'You can't fool the people at the bottom,' Mama said. 'They always know what's really going on."

In December 1944 we left Ried for good. Our destination was Hinterhör, some 40 miles east of Ried, where we were likely to be safer as the war approached its anticlimactic end. Among Nazis or their sympathizers in Ried, hostility to the 'Americans' in their midst had grown in direct proportion to the success of American arms. Although we received the same food ration cards as everyone else, the supply of food actually made available was controlled by the owner of the only grocery in town, an ardent nationalist by the name of Brummer. Sweety Degenfeld's social standing offered greater hope of protection against potential nationalist retaliation, while Mama's presence in Hinterhör might in turn offer local residents the prospects of better treatment at the hands of potentially vengeful American soldiers. Hinterhör itself was crowded with evacuees and refugees, but Sweety found space for us in the *Elmhof* nearby, a large farmstead by then also converted into living quarters for internal refugees from all over Germany, including a number of displaced Balts.

Our 40-mile trip to Hinterhör shortly before Christmas in 1944 turned into an all-night adventure, as faithfully recorded in the personal journal I started keeping, on and off, from the age of seven. Normally the trip would have taken no more than four hours, changing trains in Munich, but the destruction of the railroad facilities in and around the big city, the unreliability of rail service, and the constant threat of air raids made travel via Munich an unrealistic option. So we tried a more direct route, attempting to make our way town by town by whatever means available. Why we started so late in the day I do not know, but there was something furtive about our departure. We started off on foot at six in the evening, using Frau von Velsen's hand-pulled cart for our baggage, which included our two cats. From the neighboring village of Bichl we got an apparently pre-arranged ride by wood-fired truck (Tempy and I got to sit in the cab!) to the regional capital of Bad Tölz, where I had been taken to the hospital two-and-a-half years earlier when I had TB. From there we intended to go by train to Rosenheim, the rail hub closest to Hinterhör. We only made it as far as the nearby town of Kolbermoor, as the tracks into Rosenheim were impassable. From Kolbermoor we walked four or five miles to the next-closest station of Grosskarolinienfeld, where we children were told to go to sleep on the benches and tables in the overcrowded waiting room. At four in the morning we caught the first bus to Raubling, eight miles to the south, completing our journey to Hinterhör as we had started, on foot, at eight in the morning. The only casualties were our cats, one of whom had run away, while the other one died a few days later of what we were sure was homesickness. Ten years later, in Canaan, Connecticut, I recorded in my journal Mama's verdict on this trip. To Fritzi von Kügelgen's suggestion that they all take a trip to Germany to see everything again, Mama replied: 'I don't want to visit Berlin. And I never want to see Grosskarolinienfeld again as long as I live.' And she never did.

The Elmhof

Although we were surrounded by destruction everywhere, it was only in the last three months of the war that we felt the direct effects of a bombing raid. The Elmhof lay a bit outside the village of Rohrdorf, where we got our groceries. Betsy and I had just left the village, our hand-drawn *Leiterwagen* filled with supplies we had been instructed to fetch, when a cluster of bombs fell unexpectedly on Rohrdorf, producing the whining sound and the explosions that were quite familiar to us by then, but never so nearby (the proximity reduced the whining sound and amplified the explosions). A plume of smoke rose from the center of the village. It turned out that the bakery where we had bought bread only a few minutes before was one of the places hit. All of the people inside at the time were killed. That was, as far as I know, our closest call during the war. But on our treks between Elmhof and Hinterhör, where we still took Latin lessons (and Olaf took Greek), we saw the effects of bombs that had fallen harmlessly into the countryside, leaving only craters behind. Some had water at the bottom that eventually dried out in the course of the long, hot summer of 1945. We concluded that Rohrdorf was just a target of convenience for an isolated Allied plane anxious to drop its payload before returning to its base. There was, however, a cement factory close by, well-concealed by foliage and evergreen trees at the edge of the woods. That plant was apparently the objective of the Allied bombers, but they never managed to hit it. After the war, with rising demand for concrete for reconstruction, this factory became one of the largest and most profitable enterprises in Bavaria. The sound of aircraft was always frightening to us children, especially toward the end of the war. When we heard a plane approaching, our first reaction was to take shelter under the nearest tree. If it turned out to be a German plane, as it usually did, we felt great relief. Even in the relative tranquility of Ried, my first inclination on hearing the sound of a plane in the distance as I lay in bed at night was to beg God to save my life.

Yet the fear of death is not the hardship I associate most directly with the war. Hunger and the shortage of food also were unpleasant rather than traumatic in my recollection. We were hungry all the time and competed and connived for food, but I had never known anything different anyway for years. True, even superficial scrapes or sores on the body or limbs would not heal and became easily infected, but it was only well after the war, back in America, that I experienced the worst after-effects of malnutrition and vitamin deficiency, in my case stunted growth and an intestinal tumor resulting from the sudden excess of overly rich foods. In my mind, at least in retrospect, the war was most closely associated with two other afflictions to which all of us children fell prey at one time or another: worms and lice. The most immediate effects of both were similar: constant itching. We were told to always inspect our feces. The most common form of intestinal parasites were easily visible, squirming like maggots in pieces of rotting cheese. Some of us also had tape worms, which, if one was lucky, could be extracted through the anus, though rarely without breaking at some point, thus (at least in our worst fantasies) leaving a portion to regenerate behind.

The war came to an end for us sometime in late April or early May. We knew that the end was close when one day a retreating SS unit simply dumped in the center of Rohrdorf its hoard of everyday household goods that were virtually impossible for civilians to obtain. I particularly recall the huge stocks of scarce string and wire that suddenly became available just for the taking. We heard artillery and rifle fire in the distance, but there was no fighting or resistance in our immediate vicinity. We had packed rucksacks for each of us, hand-sewn out of sheets, with clothes, blankets, and food in case we would have to take to the hills or forests, but that turned out not to be necessary. One of the displaced aristocrats at the Elmhof, Baron von der Osten-Sacken, an elderly gentleman who lived alone on the fourth floor with his dog Treff, rode on his bicycle to meet the advancing American troops and officially surrendered the village without a fight. From the safety of our shared room we children watched the remnants of German army units with their horse-drawn equipment retreating in an obvious state of dissolution on the road that ran in front of and below the Elmhof. That night was marked by a sound entirely new to us, but soon to become very familiar: the rhythmical Doppler effect of wheeled or tracked vehicles—jeeps, trucks, and tanks—as a seemingly unending succession of American military vehicles passed through our area on the Munich-Salzburg Autobahn a few miles to the north. I recall that the end of the war left us with a huge sense of relief, even if we couldn't pinpoint the exact date when it happened. The war officially ended on my tenth birthday, May 8th (the German surrender in the West was signed on the 7th, the surrender in the East early on the 9th). We knew the war was over, of course, but it was not until later that I learned that my birthday had in fact coincided with V-E Day.

3
Our Return to America, 1945-1946

The first American relative who showed up at the Elmhof after the war (and the only one I can remember, although there were others) was Mama's first cousin, Army Captain Grenville Emmet (1909-1989). His father, Granny's brother Grenville Emmet (1877-1937), had been the American Special Envoy to the Netherlands in 1933-1934 and Special Envoy to Austria until his death in 1937. Mama's brother Nicholas Biddle (1906-1986) was a Lieutenant Commander in the Navy and still actively engaged in the war against Japan. Mama did not see him again until she returned to America the following year. Two American soldiers stationed near our village, Bill and Mack, their last names now forgotten, came to visit us at the Elmhof every Sunday in the summer of 1945, as recorded in my diary. Mack flattered Mama by telling her she looked like Katharine Hepburn. Bill, an army cook, made a proposal of marriage to Wini, as she later told me, but Wini was not tempted. Bill and Mack returned to the States in September. Other American friends at the Elmhof included the UNRRA workers Jean and Margaret, attached to the Displaced Person camp in Rosenheim. They remained good friends of ours back in America.

Our own return was delayed by the absence of a civilian government or administration as well as military red tape, apparently because Mama was still classified as an enemy alien for having been married to a German. She may also have been reluctant to leave Wini behind. As a Dutch citizen with a brother who had joined the SS her immigration would have been much more problematic than Mama's repatriation. Her brother Ronald claimed that he had never actually sworn allegiance to the Nazis, but this did not save him from prosecution in his home country after the war. We spent one more year at the Elmhof before departing on our return trip to the U.S. in June 1946. Mama and Wini took charge of converting the lawn in front of the Elmhof into a huge vegetable garden, as they had previously done in Ried. Nonetheless, food remained the most pressing problem we faced. Mama gained a life-long aversion to green tomatoes, which we harvested early to beat the frost and fried in various forms to add some vitamins to our meals. We did begin to receive Care packages and huge tins of dried eggs and dried milk from our relatives at home. Mama always shared these gifts with the increasing number of residents of the Elmhof. One new addition in the spring of 1945 was Erich, an Austrian boy about Betsy's age, who had lost his parents and his home in the fighting around Vienna. He had been picked up while wandering aimlessly in search of a place to stay by our playmate Tassilo von Winterfeldt, who was the same age and lived with his mother Tanya and their former maid Frieda with us in the building adjoining the Elmhof. Erich stayed with us for several months and participated in all our activities. We were very impressed by the toughness and worldly wisdom he had acquired as an orphan on the road.

We four American children soon established a daily routine of walking to the Autobahn to beg for chewing gum, candy, food, and, on behalf of the adults at the Elmhof (who sometimes told us not to come back until we got them them), coffee and cigarettes. Cigarettes had become the principal means of exchange in Germany at the end of the war as the German currency and postage stamps lost all value. All over the country people fought over cigarette butts in the streets and on the sidewalks. These were then stripped of their tobacco and rolled into new cigarettes. American tobacco was, of course, particularly prized for its superior quality.

On one of our first tramps to the Autobahn we encountered huge columns of German prisoners of war being marched to detention camps. I remember how, during a "latrine break," squatting soldiers answering nature's call covered the entire hillside as far as the eye could reach. Among the marching prisoners was Papa, functioning as an interpreter for the American guards, who gave him permission to come over to greet us. His American connection and command of English did gain him some privileges from his American captors, but proportionately greater hostility from those of his fellow prisoners who regarded him as a traitor or a brown-noser. In his memoirs, written toward the end of his life, Papa credited his survival during and immediately after the war to his ability at crucial times to recognize the *Mörderblick* (murderous eye) in persons who wished him ill. He prided himself on his foresight in staying out of their way.

During that spring and summer the best opportunity to get to know American soldiers and obtain hand-outs came when military vehicles broke down and parked at the side of the Autobahn to await repairs, sometimes for several days. By and large, we children were treated amicably and generously by the soldiers, some of whom were quite amazed to run into an American family in Germany. Our peculiar national status, however, apparently caused some dissension as to how friendly their deportment toward us should be. After all, the non-fraternization rule was still in place, and many of these soldiers had lost buddies to German shells and bullets in the war. While most of the GIs we encountered accepted our self-identified status as an American family stuck in Germany, extraordinary as it must have seemed to them, there were at least a few who viewed us children simply as linguistically dexterous Germans, concealing our true identities behind a good English vocabulary and pronunciation. The hostility of some of these embittered soldiers was quite palpable as, in the name of their fallen comrades, they tried to talk their buddies out of indulging us "Krauts." Such hostility was rare, but nonetheless a reaction with which we always had to reckon.

In my journal that summer of 1945 I recorded the many hikes and excursions we children took into the neighboring mountains and countryside. We went swimming in the Rabsee, about an hour away, walking west on the Autobahn. American soldiers swam there, too, including one time, to our amazement, several truckloads of African-Americans from a unit in the still segregated army. I still wrote my journal in German, although Mama would no longer accept any poems or stories as presents for her birthday or for other occasions unless they were written in English—one sign of how greatly the times had changed. Nevertheless, my poetry had its admirers among the other residents of the Elmhof, including the displaced Balts, Heddy Lieven and her sister Irene Dewitz, who encouraged my precocious literary endeavors with lavish praise. My themes now reflected the changed post-war conditions. No longer did I write about the heroic Carolingian crusade to convert the heathen Saxons to Christianity or the Ottonian victory over the Magyars on the Lechfeld near Augsburg in the year 955, all part of the nationalist lore we imbibed in the war. Instead I attempted to appease Mama by setting my stories in an imagined America, in the style of Karl May.

School was temporarily suspended after the war as the ideologically contaminated textbooks were replaced and the politically compromised teachers were "denazified" in an effort to bring democracy to Germany. In the interim we took private lessons at Hinterhör from Director Rieder, the former (and future) head of the school at Schloß Neubeuern. For a time we also attended a *Gymnasium* (college preparatory school) in Brannenburg, several miles away. Mama took us to school in the morning by horse and buggy borrowed from Hinterhör. This was always an adventure, as the horse shied at every approaching car. Fortunately there were very few cars on the back roads, at least until the arrival of the Americans. Several months after the end of the war a *Gymnasium* reopened (without textbooks) in Rosenheim. We could get there by train, although we had to walk more than two hours along the tracks to get back home, as the return train did not run until evening.

In May 1946 we paid our last visit to our paternal grandparents in Bad Reichenhall, about 50 miles to the southeast close to the Austrian border. Here Papa had settled down with his second family at the end of the war. It was in Reichenhall that I first saw, in a visit to the local cinema, the shocking footage of the British liberation of Bergen-Belsen and the mass burial, with bulldozers, of thousands of emaciated corpses. Films of Nazi atrocities were shown all over Germany as part of the Allied denazification effort. In the audience in Reichenhall there were muffled voices of outrage, disgust, and disbelief. In the back of the theatre one male voice could be heard to mutter that it was all Himmler's fault.

On 11 June 1946 at 6 in the morning we left the Elmhof for the last time. I recorded our journey in the last of my childhood diaries still written in German. All the details of where we stayed, whom we met, and what we did can be found there, but the laconic monotone does not reveal any of the emotions my siblings or I must (or may) have felt—neither joy nor sadness, excitement nor regret. I do vividly remember the bed sheet that those we left behind unfurled from the balcony at the Elmhof, bidding us farewell and god-speed.

Susanne, Olaf, Betsy, Stella, Rodi, and Tempy in Bad Reichenhall, April 1946

We travelled by truck to Munich, and from there by overcrowded trains to Lindau on the *Bodensee* (the Lake of Constance). A passenger steamer brought us to Constance the next day, where we crossed the border to Switzerland on foot, with little baggage and no money. Mama gave away her now worthless German marks to a porter who had helped us with our luggage. Olaf's German shepherd Nora, who made the whole long trip with us to America, crossed the Swiss (and later the Italian) borders on her own and rejoined us on the other side. In Kreuzlingen on the Swiss side of the border we had our first meal outside of Germany, an experience that sticks in my mind because of the delicious flavor of the unaccustomed fresh-baked white bread. As prearranged with Miss Foote, a long-time friend of the family and an associate of Carl Jung's, we travelled by taxi to Zurich and spent the night at the hotel where she lived.

According to Mama after the war, the usual transatlantic route via Hamburg or Bremerhafen was closed to us because of the huge demand for shipping to bring home thousands of returning American troops. As I understood it at the time, our stay in Switzerland was to be temporary but indefinite and would end when passage to America via an Italian port could be secured. We children were placed in a small boarding school in the Swiss alpine village of Villars, about 30 miles southeast of Lausanne in the French-speaking part of Switzerland. Mama and Wini returned to Zurich to complete preparations for our voyage. Uncle Nick wired $500 to cover the costs of our stay and the trip. While the roughly 40 pupils at Villars attended classes, we four children received lessons in French.

On 18 June 1946 our alpine idyll came to an unexpectedly sudden close. We were told to return to Zurich immediately, as our transatlantic passage had been booked. The following day we travelled from Zurich to Lugano by train (through very long tunnels, as I appreciatively recorded in my journal). On June 30th we crossed the Italian border at Chiasso by bus, we children sitting on top of the baggage strapped to the roof. We left Wini behind in Lugano. She would rejoin us In Connecticut in 1949 after securing the necessary visa. Late that evening we arrived in Genoa, where our ship, the Vulcania, was scheduled to depart on July 5th. In the intervening days we did a lot of sightseeing in the heavily damaged city. Its destruction paled, however, against the devastation of Munich or Augsburg, the German cities we had most recently seen. In my diary I noted the good food in Genoa and the welcome chance to go bathing in the sea. What I did not mention, but sticks in my mind to this day, is the raw floating sewage we had to dodge while swimming in the polluted harbor.

Our ten-day transatlantic voyage on the Vulcania included only one stop. We did not disembark at Palermo, where we docked for several hours the next day. Instead, we stood at the railing in the blistering heat and watched Sicilian youths diving in the surprisingly clear water to retrieve coins thrown to them by passengers on board. That night the weather grew stormy and all of us children got seasick the next day. This did not prevent us from admiring the view of Gibraltar, however, which we passed on the evening of July 7th. After a week on the open sea we arrived at the entrance to New York harbor at dawn on July 15th. Betsy, who had gotten up early with Mama to see the Statue of

Liberty, reported that Mama had been moved to tears. Mama's older siblings, Uncle Nick Biddle and Aunt Temple (1908-1983), met us at the dock in what must have been an emotional reunion.

Mama on the Vulcania, July 1946

The family with Mama's shipboard friend

We spent the first night at our great aunt Eleanor Emmet Lapsley's in Bedford, about an hour's drive from the city. Tempy, still following instructions based on conditions in Europe and on board ship, informed Mama that it was safe to sit on the toilets in this house! We spent the next eight weeks enjoying the hospitality of our close relatives, two weeks each at Aunt Temple's in Concord, NH, and Uncle Nick's summer home in Cohasset, MA, and the remaining four weeks with Aunt Eleanor's daughter, Nora Iselin (1907-1971) and her husband Columbus, on Martha's Vineyard. The marvelous taste and easy accessibility of ice cream was a source of wonder, but unfortunately it made me sick. Only later did I discover that this was due not (or not only) to my gorging on this novel delicacy, but to a lactose intolerance that I had apparently developed during the war. In Concord we got to know our Edmonds cousins, Nick, Liz, Ellen, and Johnny, only two years old at the time. In Cohasset and Milton, MA, we got to know our Biddle cousins, Ginny, Kitty, Liz, and Nick, Jr. Snatches of memory of that summer stick in my mind: the discovery of peanut butter, the most delicious spread I thought I had ever tasted; the snapping turtles in the pond in which we swam in Concord; listening to Stephen Foster songs for hours on end on the automatic 78 rpm record player in Milton, a technical and musical revelation to me; fishing for flounder in Cohasset; hunting on Martha's Vineyard and shedding bitter tears after killing a rabbit with a "22" borrowed from the Iselins.

On 10 September 1946 a new phase of our life was to begin. Olaf and I headed to St. Paul's School in Concord, where we were to enter the third and first forms, respectively. We only saw each other once a week, however, at our German lessons with Herr Schade, as the "lower school" was completely separate from the "upper school" at the time. Betsy was to go to the Chapin School in New York, the school from which Mama had been expelled sixteen years before. Tempy accompanied Mama to Cousin Leslie Emmet's (1877-1960) summer home in Salisbury, CT, where he would enter the third grade. We would not see each other again until Christmas, the longest separation of our young lives.

4
School and College, 1946-1956

St. Paul's was quite difficult at first because of the language adjustment. I remember there was a word whose meaning I absolutely could not grasp: "environment." I did badly on a social studies test because the conceptual peculiarity of this word was not clear to me. It was explained to me as equivalent to all human and natural surroundings, the world around us, but I could not understand the need for a separate word to replace surroundings. The German equivalent, *Umgebung* (today the preferred translation is *Umwelt*) carried no special significance. Only much later did the reason for my initial bewilderment dawn on me. The social dimension of "environment"—the dimension revealed by its contradistinction to "heredity" as a causal factor in human behavior —was literally foreign to me. In Nazi Germany, with its emphasis on blood and race, biological and hereditary factors explained all social phenomena and personal traits. For the first time I was exposed to an entirely different explanation for why people acted as they did. It took me quite a while to catch on to the importance of environment as a social (rather than purely biological) concept.

In the first marking period I was a high average student, excelling only in Latin, which I had already studied for years in Germany. In the second marking period, however, my grades soared. From then on I was usually among the top three scholars in my form, a very advantageous rank, as it was rewarded by a special holiday during the year and a Christmas vacation extended by two days. For Christmas we traveled by train and bus to Lakeville (a village in the township of Salisbury, Connecticut), where we were picked up by jeep to be delivered to Cousin Les's home on Selleck Hill in Salisbury, where Mama now lived. It was a memorable reunion. Tempy and I sat in the back of the jeep, but we could not talk to each other, as every time one of us tried to say something we involuntarily burst out laughing. The emotions were just too overpowering. Years later I was surprised that some critics of the film *Europa, Europa* viewed the famous closing scene as unlifelike and unreal. Solly and his brother Isaac could not stop laughing when they saw each other again after the war. To me that scene rang particularly true.

In the spring of my first form year at St. Paul's the intestinal blockage diagnosed as "ileitis" was discovered. It would have been discovered far sooner if I had sought treatment when my symptoms first appeared. As it was, I did not go to the infirmary until I was ordered to. My friend Bryce Walker had seen me writhing in pain during a chess game. I told him it would soon pass, it had happened many times before. Beads of sweat gathered on my face as I cramped, but after about five minutes or so the pain would abate, and things would return more or less to normal. I had been brought up in the belief that, like a good soldier, one had to learn to bear physical pain and discomfort without complaining. The measure of a person's worth was the degree of suffering and sacrifice one was willing to bear. Suffering in silence meant subordinating one's own personal comfort to the larger good of the whole—a value strongly encouraged in war-time Germany. It took me a while to understand that in America there was no stigma attached to physical weakness or to seeking medical help. The operation was successful, and the affected portions of my intestines were removed. As a bonus I was excused from all my final exams (and I have never had to worry about putting on too much weight).

Although I suffered pangs of homesickness, I enjoyed my time at St. Paul's much more than Olaf, who always felt somewhat out of place. I knew there was something quite odd about me, however. My favorite pastime was to crawl under my bed with the sports section of the newspaper and transcribe the box scores of baseball games into notebooks where I kept statistical information on teams and players I had made up. By basing this imaginary competition on the box scores of real games, I felt I was removing the arbitrary factor from games that took place only in my imagination. I could never be sure in advance which of my imaginary teams would win, what the score would be, and how each of my imaginary players would perform. The real fun would come in finding out which of my imaginary teams did best in the league standings I kept and in figuring out the batting averages of my imaginary players. At the same time I became a life-long Red Sox fan, glued to the radio (at home), listening to the play-by-play reports which in those days were still done by teletype in the case of away games. My priorities changed during hockey season, a sport greatly emphasized at St. Paul's. Here I was often the last person to leave the ice. Skating became as much of an obsession as making up baseball teams had been during the baseball season.

Our tenure at St. Paul's came to an end in 1948 due to a family quarrel, in some ways no doubt also a late consequence of the terrible war. When Mama first came back from the war, she literally didn't have a penny to her name. Until she finally got a low-paying housekeeping job in the fall of 1946, she was entirely dependent on the charity of her siblings. In a memorable five-page letter to Maria Marc in Ried in September 1946 she expressed her bitter frustration at not being able to help her old friends in Germany in any way. "I have literally not a penny to my name," she wrote, "and it might take two or three years to get my money. I have been able to buy *nothing*, but my family has given me a lot." Although both Olaf and I received half-scholarships from St. Paul's, the other half of the tuition was paid by Uncle Nick. Mama had willingly accepted her brother's offer in her mistaken assumption that her own considerable Biddle inheritance would soon become available to her. In 1948 it was still tied up in the courts due to legislation mandating the seizure of German assets during the war. By her marriage Mama had automatically become a German citizen, without, however, renouncing her American citizenship. In the event, the litigation dragged on for years and when her inheritance finally came through in 1951, most of it had been absorbed by legal fees. Uncle Nick would certainly have been willing to continue paying our tuition in 1948, but he made a tactical mistake by revealing to Mama, apparently in an off-hand remark, that it was all "Morris money" anyway. Morris was the family of his wife, our Aunt Virginia (1907-1990). While Mama was willing to accept "Biddle money" for the education of her sons and daughter, she absolutely refused to accept financial assistance from her sister-in-law, whose political, social, and cultural outlook was very different from her own. As Aunt Temple, whose fabled generosity was also frequently rebuffed, later remarked, "The trouble with your mother is that she doesn't know how to accept presents."

The immediate consequence of Mama's proud renunciation was that we entered a period of dire poverty. She was not, however, too proud to do whatever she could to raise a family of four children on her own. With a new family of his own and a devalued German currency, Papa was in no position to provide any financial help, even if Mama had requested it, which she didn't. Mama worked as a housekeeper for John and Martha Briscoe and their two sons in Lakeville for $35 a week (later raised to $40). An early riser throughout her life, Mama chose to work from 6 a.m. to 2 p.m. so she could be home when we got back from school. To commute to the Briscoe farm, about 20 minutes away, she used a 1929 Model T Ford that had to be cranked by hand to start. Sometimes, especially in cold weather, it took her fifteen minutes or more just to start the car, a labor-intensive ritual that we overheard from the warmth of our beds. On the stove she left us a big pot of oatmeal porridge that constituted our daily breakfast. We three older children chipped in by taking after-school and weekend jobs, if only to earn enough money for our own clothing and personal expenses. Olaf earned the most by working as a garage hand and later a store clerk. Betsy did babysitting, and I, ineligible for a regular job at age 13, did housework for three elderly ladies, mopping the kitchen and porch on my hands and knees, vacuuming the carpets, raking leaves, and doing other household and yard chores for 35 cents an hour. Even nine-year-old Tempy earned money, cleaning storm windows. Later he found a much more lucrative source of income as a caddy at the Hotchkiss School golf course.

Meanwhile our own dingy home was often a mess. We rented a small two-bedroom apartment on the second floor of an electrician's home in Lakeville. There was no dining room and Mama slept on a couch in the living room. Making matters worse, we had a succession of cats that were not properly housebroken, one of which, an albino, we gave the well-earned name of *Weisse Scheisse*. Mama blamed the dirt and the clutter on us children (in a memorable fit of rage because Olaf had failed to make his bed, she threw his mattress out the window), but in fact she was probably just as much to blame. All her life she surrounded herself with animals (not just cats and dogs, but later chickens and goats as well), indifferent to the fact that as a consequence of her love of animals the interiors of her homes soon came to resemble stables. No less a philosopher than Immanuel Kant once said that people clean their houses for visitors, not for themselves. Well, the good opinion of conventional society would never have been enough incentive for Mama to change her preferred way of life. In her late seventies in Albany, Vermont, when Olaf offered to hire someone to help her with cleaning chores, Mama retorted, "I don't care if this house is never cleaned again."

In September 1948 we started high school at Housatonic Valley Regional High School, the first regional high school in New England, opened in 1939, serving the widely dispersed towns of Salisbury, Falls Village, Canaan, Sharon, Cornwall, and Kent in the northwest corner of Connecticut (the name of our school newspaper was *The Northwest Corner*). At age 13 I was one of the youngest members of my freshman class, as I had already been the youngest student at St. Paul's in 1946-1947. Olaf, on the other hand, was one of the oldest members of his class, as he was forced to repeat his sophomore year. This led to the anomaly that Betsy, who had completed her sophomore year in New York, was a year ahead of Olaf in school. Tempy continued his schooling in Salisbury, entering the fifth grade.

The most memorable event of 1948 was the presidential election in November. Mama stayed up all night listening to the returns on the radio, despite her distaste for the commentary of H. V. Kaltenborn, who clearly supported the heavily favored Republican challenger Thomas Dewey. The election was not decided until early afternoon the following day. School was interrupted by our principal Dr. Stoddard's announcement over the public address system that Truman had won the state of California and thereby the majority of electoral votes. We were among the few families in that generally conservative area to celebrate this unexpected triumph. However, had I known then what I know now, my sympathies would have been with Henry Wallace, who, like so many progressive candidates in elections to come, never had a realistic chance to win.

To celebrate the tenth anniversary of the founding of the school, Eleanor Roosevelt came to speak. Mama knew Mrs. Roosevelt from her childhood (her father had actually been one of Eleanor's suitors before FDR made the running). Apparently Mama asked Mrs. Roosevelt to intercede with the State Department to facilitate Wini's immigration. Whether as a result of this intercession, or simply because of the passage of time, Wini was finally able to rejoin us in Connecticut in 1949. She got a job at Salisbury School, a private school for boys, where she was also given a small apartment to live.

To save money in the summer of 1949 Mama decided to sublet our apartment and camp out on a two-acre plot of land on Farnum Road in Lakeville that the Briscoes were willing to sell to us on a generous long-term installment plan. Here on the isolated hilltop site about two miles from town, named Thornhill by us in a rough translation of "Stachelberg", Olaf built a 200 sq. ft. lean-to shack on a four-cornered cinderblock foundation. The lumber sufficed only for walls that were about waist-high.

The shack built by Olaf on Thornhill in summer 1949

To protect against the weather we hung ponchos from the eaves of the slanting roof. The advantage of this arrangement was that we didn't have to worry about windows, as the ponchos were usually rolled up during the day, except in very inclement weather. We did not have to worry about the lack of privacy, either, as we were surrounded by forest (which also served as our toilet area) and there were no neighbors in sight. Mama and Wini, who joined us for the summer, slept inside Olaf's home-made shack while we children slept in the narrow space under the floorboards in sleeping bags or out in the open. We had no running water or electricity. One consequence was that the barber in Lakeville refused to cut my hair because it was so dirty. He was afraid of damaging his scissors, and I didn't have the money to pay for a shampoo. So we lived from the end of school in June until the end of September when we returned to our apartment above the Stilsons, and Wini went back to Salisbury School. The following summer, in 1950, we had a more weather-proof shack built by a local carpenter who actually put in a window. By then we had saved up enough money to buy army-surplus pup tents for us children. Except for the mosquitoes and occasional leaks and mud puddles during heavy rains, it was actually a lot of fun.

Our shack on Thornhill, summer of 1950

During that summer of 1950 the Briscoes started construction on a small 1½ story Dutch colonial style house with three dormer windows that would become our first "permanent" home in the fall of 1950. The indoor plumbing and electrical appliances seemed like the height of luxury to us. The living room (with fireplace), kitchen, and bathroom were on the ground floor, as were separate rooms for Mama and Wini. We four children slept upstairs, with Betsy having a room of her own, Olaf and I sharing a room, and Tempy sleeping in the narrow hall-like space at the top of the stairs. To augment our income we took on the job of delivering the Sunday *New York Times* to its local subscribers (one of whom, as I boasted to my friends, was the celebrated harpsichordist Wanda Landowska, who lived in Lakeville). For this purpose Mama acquired a second-hand, four-wheel-drive jeep truck which Olaf drove while I assisted him in distributing the papers. We had to get up at 3 a.m. on Sundays to put together the many different sections of the paper (some of which had arrived earlier in the week) and to write the names of the recipients on the front pages before loading the papers on to the truck. This was a time-consuming task as there were nearly a hundred subscribers in our delivery area, yet we usually managed to get most of the papers delivered between 6 and 9 a.m. More difficult at times was collecting the money owed by subscribers, which was also part of our task. We carried on this business for two years, until Mama's inheritance came through. When Olaf went off to college in the fall of 1951, I took over driving the truck, once getting into trouble for allowing my young assistant, "Tuffy" Herter, to stand on the running board to save time between deliveries.

Mama looked for other ways to augment our income. While still at the Stilsons' she hit upon the idea of starting a flower business, as there was no florist in town at the time. On the weekends either Olaf or I would get up very early and accompany her to the wholesaler in Hartford or New York to pick up the flowers which we would then convert into floral arrangements at home to fill orders taken during the week. These trips were especially tense in winter as our car had practically no heat to protect the flowers from freezing. The other big challenge was Mama's lack of training in how to make wreaths and other more elaborate floral arrangements, though that didn't stop her from accepting large orders for weddings or funerals. Lack of knowledge was sometimes an advantage, because by forcing her to improvise with laborious sewing and stitching methods, she was able to turn out products of higher quality than those made with foam rubber or other time-saving expedients by conventional florists. Wini eventually filled the knowledge gap by completing a correspondence course and becoming quite expert at the floral trade. In 1951, when her inheritance finally came through, Mama partnered with Wini in opening a flower shop in a tiny two-story building on Main Street in Salisbury village. Mama soon tired of sitting in the shop waiting for customers (as she described it) and turned the business over to Wini, making a present of the building to her on the birth of Wini's son John in October 1951. Under Wini's proprietorship the shop flourished. She sold the shop for a nice profit in 1978 and the right to continue living in her upstairs quarters until her death (which occurred in 2007).

High school was easy and fun, despite my sense of insecurity, a result not only of my retarded physical development, but of other issues as well. One such issue was my name. I was formally enrolled as John R. Stackelberg and therefore was generally addressed as John, throughout high school and college. I didn't think of myself as John, but was much too shy to buck the overwhelming tide of convention. At home I was called Rodi (or Lodi by my siblings, because Olaf had trouble pronouncing the R when he was a toddler), short for the German Roderich, the only first name on my birth certificate issued in Munich in May 1935. The first name John was apparently added by Mama at my baptism, after Aunt Temple's husband, John Edmonds, who became my godfather. Papa claimed to have been taken fully by surprise, another chapter, no doubt, in the ongoing marital wars, which were also about our competing maternal and paternal heritages. For me it complicated the questions of personal (and national) identity that have troubled me all my life. Another complication was Mama's decision in 1948 no longer to use the adjunct "von" in our name, which in Germany indicated hereditary nobility. Not only was this a concession to American egalitarianism and post-war anti-German sentiment, but it also simplified matters by preempting the incorrect American practice of alphabetizing our name under V (for Von Stackelberg) rather than under S, where it belongs.

At the Timmons Grove on Lake Wononscopomoc, summber of 1950

While still at the Stilsons' in the late 1940s, Mama sometimes read out loud to us from the Dickens classics, from *The Fairchild Family*, and once from Oscar Wilde's *Ballad of Reading Gaol.* For herself she read a book she enjoyed and praised called *The Mature Mind.* We listened to the radio most evenings. Tempy's favorite show was *The Lone Ranger*, always introduced by Rossini's famous *Wilhelm Tell Overture.* We also listened to Sam Spade and on Sundays to *Your Weekly Hit Parade*, keeping score on how a particular song had progressed from the previous week. *Goodnight Irene* hit the top of the hit parade in 1950 and became my favorite song. In the course of the 1950s I would wear out three successive long-playing records of the Weavers. We also listened to Burl Ives singing folk and country songs.

On the long bus rides to high school I daydreamed about writing a book on world affairs from the perspective of a teenager, but, of course, I never followed through on this idea. High school offered too many extra-curricular diversions for any serious project like that. Olaf played football, advancing to the position of fullback when he proved to the coach that he could run just as fast as the team star, "Buka" Thurston. Coach Ben Bedini (1921-2008), a young man recently out of Springfield College, asked me to become team manager, a role I gladly accepted, since I was much too small and frail to play any sport. Yet I was very interested in sports, which I covered for our local paper, *The Lakeville Journal.* My models were the sports writers of the *New York Times.* I also listened to Marty Glickman on the radio, who proclaimed every made basket "good like Needex", the orange drink chain that sponsored the broadcasts. I also kept the official score for our Lakeville semi-pro baseball team, where one bright Sunday afternoon in June 1950, sitting in the dugout, I heard of the North Korean invasion of the South. The most exciting sports moment came one afternoon in early October 1951, while working an after-school job at the Miners' horse farm on the Lakeville-Lime Rock road. Here I heard "the shot heard round the world" when Bobby Thompson's homerun with two men on against the Brooklyn Dodgers at the Polo Grounds in the bottom of the ninth put the Giants into the World Series against the Yankees, which, however, the Giants predictably lost in those years of Yankee dominance.

While Olaf was still in school, I was often referred to as "little Olaf." There was some justification for this as I followed him in virtually all his high school offices, from editor of the school newspaper to founding member and president of our successful high school chess club. Unexpectedly, our chess team beat all the prestigious private schools in the area, including the

Hotchkiss, Kent, and South Kent teams (Salisbury School, as I recall, did not have a team at the time). My best friend, Bob Oliver, played third board on our team. Betsy, who already graduated in 1950, decided to take a postgraduate year before going to college at Barnard. This gave me the opportunity to draw the biggest laugh at our Junior Assembly in spring 1951 by following up my recitation of the comparative virtues of the freshman, sophomore, junior, and senior classes (juniors, of course, emerging as the best) with the comment, "postgraduates don't count." I also was quite proud of a joke I came up with on McArthur's dismissal as commander of UN forces in Korea (for wanting to extend the war into China), which had happened a few days earlier. In a mock newscast I announced, "Word has just been received that General McArthur has joined the Air Force. President Truman told him to go fly a kite!"

To my great relief Mama was able to pay for my tuition, room, and board at Harvard from 1952 to 1956, which in those days amounted to only $600 a year, but would have been unaffordable, if Mama's inheritance had not finally come through. Her first cousin, Pauline Emmet (1906-1983), daughter of Granny's brother Grenville (1877-1937) and his wife, our Aunt Pauline (1879-1947), generously paid for Olaf's tuition at MIT. Both Olaf and I were responsible for all our personal expenses, including clothing, textbooks, transportation, student fees, and pocket money. Olaf already held down a full-time summer job in 1949. In the summer of 1950 he began a lawn-mowing business, which I eventually took over in 1953. The summer before I went off to college in 1952 I worked full-time at our weekly newspaper, *The Lakeville Journal*, for whom I had covered local sports and written a weekly column entitled "Housatonic Highlights" – high school news from a student's perspective – for several years. Much as I enjoyed it, I found out that I wasn't cut out for a career in journalism, despite having listed as my greatest ambition in our high school yearbook, "to write for the *New York Times*."

Betsy (right) and her friend Brigitte Hanf, modeling for the Lakeville Journal, 1951

My articles in the Lakeville Journal drew praise, but I soon was told (and discovered for myself) that it took me too long to complete them. An obsessive-compulsive perfectionism and a chronic tendency to procrastinate (otherwise known as laziness) made me unsuited for newspaper work, a judgment confirmed by my failure to stick out the long and arduous trial period for membership on the editorial board of the daily *Harvard Crimson*. This required not just facility in writing, but physical stamina, enterprise, flexibility, and ability to make quick practical decisions—qualities in which I was sadly lacking.

So it was off to college in September 1952 in Olaf's 1941 Chevy, affectionately named Coogy, which he had bought from his earnings. I found Harvard quite daunting and was rather embarrassed to be referred to as a man, in the orientation addresses by sundry officials, rather than as the boy that I was, not yet having achieved my full growth or begun to shave. At least my voice had changed, which to my consternation didn't happen until my junior year in high school. I had excelled academically in high school, but Harvard was a different matter. I remember my shock and despair at getting the first C in my life, on a short paper on St. Augustine for my Social Science class. My sense of inadequacy was aggravated by the fact that I thought the paper was quite good. It took a while to adjust to Harvard's more rigorous standards. It also took me a while to understand that no one, no matter how brilliant or conscientious, could possibly complete all the assignments, required and recommended, on the course reading lists without ending up in the infirmary (where in fact I did land for a short spell after an ill-advised all-nighter to complete a paper in my junior year). My greatest handicap was my reluctance to speak up in class, even in small and informal tutorial seminars, unless called upon, which always induced a pathological anguish, lest I make a fool of myself. In my freshman year I also got drunk for the first (but certainly not the last) time in my life at a Weld Hall party held at Cronin's, where mere verbal assurances were the only proof required to convince the management that its student patrons were indeed 21 or over.

Despite my feelings of inadequacy and isolation, the positive experiences at Harvard far outweighed the negative ones. I decided to concentrate in History and Lit, with an emphasis on German literature (though not without some residual guilt at so shamelessly taking advantage of my native language skills). I didn't always understand, but certainly enjoyed, the lectures of John Finley and I. A. Richards in Hum[anities] 2, delivered to a class of many hundreds of students in Sanders Hall, the biggest auditorium on campus. Some lectures were more of an ordeal. William Langer used to sit and read his lectures, and this at 8 in the morning! I was always fighting to stay awake, but managed an A in his course nonetheless. Much more enjoyable was Crane Brinton's morning class in intellectual history, affectionately called "Breakfast with Brinton." His informal, conversational style made it hard to take notes, but easy to stay awake! Olaf made the short trip from MIT twice a week in fall semester 1953 to hear McGeorge Bundy hold forth on American foreign policy. He was a Republican at the time (and a Yalie to boot), but his lectures, always delivered to an overflowing crowd in the Severs lecture hall, were enthralling, if usually more for their eloquent articulation than their rather conventional centrist ideas. One of my tutors was Richard Pipes, still a teaching fellow at the time, a bit intimidating, but quite supportive as well. I remember the totally unwarranted pride that I felt when he pronounced Heinrich Heine a much better poet than Lord Byron. Later I concluded that the inexplicable unease that I sometimes felt in his presence was not only caused by his high expectations, but also by his ingrained conservatism, which eventually surfaced in his interpretation of the Russian Revolution as a totally illegitimate Leninist coup without any genuine popular component whatsoever. My most stimulating course at Harvard was probably Harry Levin's "Proust, Joyce, and Mann," later to transmute into "Proust, Joyce, and Kafka." I also felt a sympathetic affinity with Levin when I learned that he often experienced severe stage fright before delivering his finely crafted lectures. Bob Oliver came to visit and confirmed the uniqueness of Harvard to me by pronouncing the atmosphere at Harvard "much more intellectual" than at Cornell, where he was going to college.

Yet I had the gnawing feeling that I wasn't living up to my potential, as expressed in this entry in my journal at the end of my junior year on 8 June 1955:

> I am writing on "the morning after." It is a gray, dark day; Paul [Russell] has left for his grandmother's [in Belmont, MA], and Sy [Goldstaub] has gone home [to West New York, NJ]. I am staying for Olaf's commencement.
>
> I am not writing with spontaneous zest, but because I feel I ought to. For one thing, the book, which I "rediscovered" as I was cleaning up yesterday, is so clean and inviting, it demands to be written in. I have a gnawing feeling that I ought to leave some kind of a record of day by day thought and action, just so I won't feel it has all been wasted. Why did I suddenly give up writing last January? Many reasons: for one thing, it meant considerable exertion because the book would lose its purpose if it were vapid, disorganized, just a catalogue of what I had for breakfast on such and such a day. It is difficult to give coherent expression to incoherent ideas or attitudes. In the mind these ideas are enough to motivate conduct, but on paper they look empty and silly if they aren't systematically expounded. Furthermore, I realized that I could not be completely frank. Many isolated impressions run through my mind which I could never bring myself to put down. I thought this would completely destroy the value of the book, and indeed make the whole project pretentious, artificial, contrived—as if I were writing it for others to read instead of for my own enjoyment and benefit. I have changed my mind. Instead of trying to bare my soul, I will only try to collect experiences, eventful episodes, as I did in my German childhood diaries. My soul I have to carry with me anyway, but experiences are soon forgotten.
>
> I look back to the year just completed with mixed feelings. In a way I profited more by this one year than by any previous single year. I read some of the greatest German literature: *Faust*, Lessing's plays, *Zauberberg*, Kafka's novels— and Joyce's *Ulysses* and Proust's long novel. But I read them under pressure, in haste, and I can't say that I enjoyed even most

> of them. And I am still languishing in Group 3 despite my resolve to get straight A's this year. My papers were especially disappointing. They took the most horrendous effort and were not nearly as good as I know I can do them. My mark in Professor Schneider's graduate course depended solely on my paper. I could easily have gotten an A if I had been willing to exert myself. I really don't think I care about marks as such; but insofar as they reflect my ability I do care. I hate to think of myself as a "B" student. Right now I think that I am best suited for some kind of academic vocation; and yet if I can't do excellent work as a student, I wonder whether I will be able to as a scholar. I have no doubt I could if I pushed myself, but how am I going to push myself to push myself?

Unfortunately, my senior year confirmed my pessimistic self-analysis. It is not too much to say that I had "senioritis" all year—a condition that usually doesn't afflict students until the late spring of their senior year. To anyone who asks what I learned in my senior year in college, my honest answer would have to be, "to play bridge." When Paul Russell joined Sy Goldstaub and me as a third roommate at the beginning of our junior year we were allocated a large ground-floor suite in the main entry of Adams House on the corner of Mt. Auburn and Plympton Streets. Diagonally across Mt. Auburn Street was the *Lampoon*, where John Updike was turning out his cartoons, ribald poetry, and highly entertaining prose. Just up the road on Plympton Street was the *Crimson*, where Sy had successfully negotiated the rigorous requirements for membership. One of Adams House's advantages was its close location to the Yard. As a result of its splendidly convenient location as much as anything else, Adams C-5 came to be the gathering place for all our friends.

Sy and I had met at an election eve party in Weld Hall in November 1952 and immediately hit it off as ardent and disappointed Adlai Stevenson partisans. We roomed together in Adams D-44 our sophomore year. Sy was involved in numerous activities and enterprises, including running his own paperback newsstand in the entry to the Student Union in his freshman year and in the entry to Adams House in subsequent years. A government major, Sy would go on to Harvard Law School in the fall of 1956 and a career as a criminal defense attorney. I was a much more sedentary type, lingering over long mealtime conversations with Paul Russell, another Weld Hall resident whom I didn't really get to know until my sophomore year in Adams House. Paul was a philosophy major with a great interest in psychology as well. He would later combine these interests in his career as an idiosyncratic and innovative psychiatrist with a large private practice. I remember being quite overwhelmed by both the power of his intellect and the warmth of his personality. So impressed was I at the time that I thought I could easily spend my life in service to such a great man. Here is what I wrote about him in my journal in August 1955, after Tempy and I, returning home from a trip to Canada, dropped in unexpectedly at the Russells' summer home in Turner, Maine:

> Paul and Arlie [Paul's younger sister, the later Arlie Hochschild, a writer and sociology professor at Berkeley] were home and received us with shouts of surprise. Mrs. Russell asked us to spend the weekend. We called Mama and got permission after the customary complaints. Then we visited Devil's Den, roller-skated, played miniature golf, swam, worked a little on repairs on the barn, played ping-pong and ate profusely. It was a thoroughly enjoyable weekend. Paul's sociability, consideration, and intelligent conversation make him very enjoyable company. His main asset is an un-ebbing interest and openness—he is the perfect listener. He is interested in almost everything that is said, and he doesn't either overwhelm with talk or sit silently. He is the kind of person out of whom you get proportionately as much as you put in. That is, you can disregard him, and say only a few pleasantries, and you will get a few pleasantries in return. Or you can sit and chatter to him about yourself, and you will get a receptive audience. Or you can probe deeper, and inquiringly discuss, deal with a problem or topic with all the resolution you can muster, and you will be sure to get an equal effort, which usually produces a superior result, from Paul. That is why it is always satisfying and usually rewarding to talk to Paul.
>
> Arlie is quite different. She, like most people, is likely to guide conversation to the point she wants it, instead of being stimulated, like Paul, by the points to which conversation has been directed by other people. These things aren't all black and white. But where Paul is flexible, Arlie is constant; where Paul is vacillating, Arlie is decisive; where Paul is open to suggestion, Arlie is closed to it. I am not comparing them on equal levels, of course. Arlie, being four years younger, is not as mature, her character is not fully molded yet. Nor does she share Paul's deep intellectuality—for

> Paul everything is finally an intellectual problem, even human problems which he professes must be treated "humanly" and not abstractly. His love for math, especially geometry, is no accident. It is brought to bear on psychological problems as well, although here he is not dealing with angles, etc. The universe must be Euclidean, the human being must be happy and successful.

Paul had what some might consider an overly fastidious side as well, which came out in his disapproval of the running bridge game that had established itself in our suite some time after the start of our senior year. The game would start around noon, after morning classes, and sometimes ran until late at night, with an ever-changing cast of participants. Sy occasionally played, and I could almost always be persuaded to sit in if a fourth was needed. Our most accomplished player and my mentor at the game was Dick Shader, later a prominent psychiatrist at Tufts University. When I saw him again in the early 1960s, I remember my amazement that he had been able to give up the game so as not to risk disharmony in his marriage. Another enthusiastic player was Gordon Goles, later a geologist at the University of Oregon who specialized in the investigation of rocks from the surface of the moon. Other regulars were the irrepressible, chain-smoking Bob Ausnit , whom I visited at his palatial family home in Sharon, Connecticut, during vacations; Don Blaufox, who went on to an immensely successful career at the Albert Einstein College of Medicine; and Peter Noerdlinger, an aspiring astrophysicist from Denver. We played for a tenth of a cent per point just to keep people honest in their bidding. It was a lot of fun, but also—at least for me—an irresistible distraction from academic assignments. Even Paul was not immune to the procrastinations to which our endless games gave rise. To my amazement he read Kant's entire *Critique of Pure Reason* in a single night, announcing with dazed assurance in the morning that he had seen "truth".

In Adams C-5 we also spent many hours talking about the latest sequels *Franny* and *Zooey* in J. D. Salinger's (1919-2010) ongoing chronicle of the Glass family in the *New Yorker.* Salinger's preoccupation with how to live authentically struck just the right note for our generation (or at least for me), worried as we always seemed to be that we were living by standards imposed on us by outside social expectations rather than by our genuine inner needs and wants. We were quite aware in the mid-1950s that we were living in a particularly conformist and un-heroic age, later to be labeled by its critics as the "silent" or "strait-jacketed generation". Salinger perfectly captured the sense of personal crisis precipitated by the fear that in the seductively easy pursuit of money and professional success we were giving up higher, more important, and ultimately more fulfilling ways of living. We did not yet know at the time that Salinger would eventually live out his values by giving up writing entirely and withdrawing into total privacy in rural New Hampshire.

In my junior year I was bitten by the culture bug, which induced a temporary preoccupation with—and eventually a lasting love for—classical, or more specifically, Romantic, music. Using the bounteous resources of the well-stocked Adams House library, I checked out records every evening and played them over and over. My favorites were Beethoven and Brahms and the tone poems of Richard Strauss. To the occasional distress of my friends, I became a proselytizer, forcing them to listen to my favorites again and again. For Olaf the *Eroica* would invariably bring up memories of visits to Adams C-5. Paul was able to impress his family by immediately identifying Shubert's *Great Symphony in C* (his own particular favorite) on the radio—an achievement he credited to my influence. I also learned from the more expansive tastes of my friends. Gordon Goles introduced me to the melancholy strains of Villa-Lobos and the seductive charms of Kurt Weill. In the spring of my senior year, we interrupted our bridge game to attend a memorable Lowell House performance of *The Threepenny Opera,* transforming a mundane weekend into one of the highlights of my college career.

Meanwhile, circumstances were also changing at home. Mama had invested the remainder of her inheritance in a huge and heavily mortgaged dairy farm in the neighboring town of Canaan. We moved to the farm in June 1954, just in time to celebrate Betsy's wedding to David Rothenberg in grand style, two weeks after Olaf married his high school sweetheart and MIT classmate, Cora Sleighter, in Kent, CT, on August 24. Despite our misgivings about the scale of the enterprise she was taking on, Mama would not be dissuaded from her goal of pursuing farming as a vocation. Here is how I described the prospects of the farm in my journal while home for Christmas vacation in December 1954:

> Approximately 45 cows are milking at present. The barn is full, however—every stanchion is in use, and heifers, goats, and horses roam about at will. Milk production is somewhat over 2,000 pounds every two days. The farm seems to be prospering, although there are many signs of

general inefficiency—the big truck has no battery—it can apparently only be used if the battery from the Massey Harris [tractor]is transferred; the chain on the manure spreader has to be secured by bailing wire; there is never enough wood; wet feeding is sloppily done— in two small wheelbarrows because the cart designed for the purpose has a flat tire; and most of all, there is no general plan of action. Things are done "on the spur of the moment," according to temporary whims. Thus Bill and Danny [hired hands] are often excused from work in order to go hunting; no permanent records are kept, as far as I can see; the barn is cleaned, the dishes washed, wood is cut—not according to a "program," but as the urgencies of particular times require. One day Tempy and I clean the barn, another day Mama and Danny, or Danny and Bill, and so on. Milking times are arbitrarily set. Necessary things are rarely bought in advance of when they are needed—for instance, we are all out of fertilizer for the barn right now, and have been for some days.

Of course, this free and easy system of farm management has a number of advantages over a rigidly planned system. For one thing, employer-employee relationship is here, I think, just about as good as possible, given the individuals and circumstances involved. Bill and Danny are both very likable, but as workers hard to handle—especially over a period of several months or more. Both are temperamental, both drink—and neither of them, particularly Danny, is reliable—or at least they never have been up to now. Mama gives them pretty much a free hand—she treats them with affection and sincere interest, as friends rather than employees, with never a hint of command or condescension. [She also liked Bill's politics, whose description of Eisenhower she cited: "He thinks his shit don't stink."] It has worked remarkably well. Both men, notorious for their inability to hold down jobs for more than a few weeks, are happy here, and work steadily, if slowly. I think Danny will be here for the rest of the winter at least, or until he gets a job as a painter again. Bill, I'll bet, will still be here next Christmas.

Mama, I think, is very happy on the farm. She probably would be less so if she had to act according to specific plans, or if she had to promulgate these plans. She is much happier pursuing vague long-range goals, often dreams (goats), while working out day-by-day problems as they arise. She has always advocated resiliency and flexibility in life—and on the farm she puts it into practice. Whether this somewhat haphazard approach precludes real success remains to be seen. Right now the farm, run in plodding fashion, is profitable. But in the long run, the lack of know-how and absence of long-range planning may tell. Fortunately, it would take gross inefficiency or some unforeseeable catastrophe to render the farm unprofitable, so great are the earnings. And since Mama is a great worker, and always will be, it is unlikely that the farm will fail for a while.

With Danny Ashman on the Canaan farm

Alas, my prognosis was wrong. The farm failed within four years. The "unforeseeable catastrophe" did in fact occur when almost the entire herd came down with TB. Before that the workers had already quit or been let go, and in his senior year in high school, 1955-1956, Tempy had to do the milking before going to school in the morning and right after school in the afternoon, adversely affecting both his academic performance and his social life. Alerted to Mama's plight, Uncle Nick retained our cousin John Rand, a lawyer, to see what could be done. Alas, he only made things worse by calling Mama's financial troubles to the attention of her many creditors. As a result they all demanded payment at once, leaving no option but legal bankruptcy. Of everything she had invested in the farm, all that was left in the fall of 1958 was enough for a down payment on an isolated 175-acre farmstead without livestock or indoor plumbing in northern Vermont.

On the Canaan farm, 1954

Deterioration of conditions on the farm led to the break-up of the long and close family relationship with Wini, who lived with Mama and Tempy on the farm but commuted daily to Salisbury to run the flower store full time. In the winter of 1957-1958 she felt compelled to move in with John and Charlotte Rand (John was Cousin Les's great-nephew, the son of Cousin Bay [the well-known artist Ellen Emmet Rand {1875-1941}]) because of the lack of wood for the wood furnace, although Tempy did gamely try to keep up the supply on rushed weekend visits from Storrs, CT, where he had enrolled at UConn after graduating from high school in 1956. Wini decided she could not risk the health of her young son (fathered in 1951 by Fritzi's husband Werner von Kügelgen) by staying on the farm in Canaan another winter, unless conditions changed. Aunt Temple, who had just moved with her family from Concord to a large farm house in Andover, Massachusetts, invited Wini to move in with them. This, of course, was the worst move she could make. Mama never forgave what she regarded as a breach of loyalty. Wini did return to Connecticut a few weeks later, but now it was to a small apartment created in the attic above the flower store in Salisbury. Here she lived for more than 40 years, raising her son (whose godfather I had become at Wini's request) and running her ever more prosperous business. She also took up painting with considerable success that included several exhibitions in New York, beginning in the late 1960s.

The gathering clouds at home seemed to parallel my own downhill slide in my senior year. In stark contrast to a long paper I wrote on Beethoven in my junior year (specifically, on his retraction of his dedication of the *Eroica* to Napoleon), for which I combed the Widener stacks for literally hundreds of documentary references, I limited the number of secondary sources I cited in the annotated bibliography of my honors thesis on Friedrich Schiller to exactly one—a self-limitation that one of my readers, Howard Hugo, pronounced as "excessively chaste." This was in part a consciously rebellious gesture on my part, deliberately rejecting the time-honored student practice of padding bibliographies with works one had never read or which had played no part in forming the paper. But it also reflected the fact that the argument I made in my thesis was generated by my tutor, Harlan Hanson, and did not originate with me. It was a critique of Schiller's aesthetic idealism as potentially authoritarian, even if the ideal that Schiller extolled was ostensibly the "state of freedom." It was an argument that in some ways anticipated my much later dissertation and book on "völkisch idealism," the moralistic urge to regenerate the world and cleanse it of its materialistic impurities, but I had not yet made this argument my own. Perhaps I had not yet outgrown the Schillerian dualism of mind or spirit and matter, the quasi-religious outlook that had permeated my childhood in Germany. It took a while to get used to utilitarian American pragmatism and the far greater significance of popular market forces in determining American values than the prescriptive ideals of European high culture.

By their senior year most of my friends and classmates had long since made up their minds what careers to pursue, but I still didn't know what to do. My good friend Dick Shader admonished me to sit down for at least half an hour to think about my future. Ever since my childhood in Germany (where *Dichter* (poet) traditionally ranked as the highest calling) I had wanted to be a writer, but was aware, though not quite ready to admit, that neither my talent nor my perseverance would be enough to achieve such an unrealistic goal. In the end I chose the path of least resistance, deciding simply to continue in graduate school what I had been doing for so many years in college. The choice of German language and literature was an obvious and easy choice as well. To the puzzlement of the young graduate fellows in Adams House, who couldn't understand why I would not prefer to stay at Harvard, I chose to pursue my graduate studies at Columbia. I hoped that a change of scenery would cure me of the indolence and indecision that plagued my last year in college. But as so often in life, things worked out rather differently than planned or anticipated.

Tempy was the only member of my family to attend my commencement in Cambridge. Olaf had moved to Minneapolis to pursue a PhD in mathematics at the University of Minnesota, before being drafted out of graduate school by our local Litchfield County draft board later that year. Mama had already by then become averse to leaving her home turf for any but the most exceptional reason. "She's always the life of the party," Tempy once said, "but she's rarely at the party."

With Sy Goldstaub in front of Adams House on graduation day, June 1956

The young junior senator from Massachusetts John F. Kennedy was our commencement speaker that year. But it was a very hot day, and Tempy and I chose to go swimming at Revere Beach instead, before heading back to the farm in Canaan for a summer of hard work.

5
New York City, 1956-1958

Returning to the farm in Canaan for the summer after graduation from college in June 1956 was not my preferred choice. I was ready finally to leave home, and in retrospect that is probably what I should have done. I had long envied Olaf his independence. He stopped coming home summers as soon as he got to college in 1951, working a variety of jobs, including one driving a Howard Johnson ice cream truck in Boston. Olaf, however, was not dependent on Mama for his tuition. The arrangement I reached with Mama in June 1956 was that she would pay my tuition for graduate school at Columbia in the fall in return for my working on the farm all summer. Having no real insight into her financial affairs, which she divulged to no one, I did not realize that the farm was already in serious financial difficulties at the time.

The summer of 1956 sticks in my memory as a season of grueling farm work. In this our third summer on the farm Tempy and I, with help from Mama, did all of the milking, cleaning, and haying, including mowing the grass, raking and baling the hay with our machinery, and—with some outside help—transporting the baled hay back to the barn, transferring the bales to the hayloft via conveyor belt, and stacking them in the loft. I also remember the summer of 1956 for listening, not without self-reproach for giving in to such a low-brow temptation, to the music of Elvis Presley, especially *Don't Be Cruel.* I had never heard such immediacy and undisguised sensuality in song before and would not have a similar experience (without the same self-reproach, to be sure) until hearing Bob Dylan for the first time five years later.

In September, after an end-of-the-summer visit to the Russells in Washington, DC, I was off to New York for graduate school in the German Department at Columbia. However, it was not a career decision to which I was sufficiently committed. I came to exactly that conclusion in a long introspective entry in my journal on 23 October 1956:

> Why am I in grad school? At the end of my senior year I had intended to either get a job or go into the army. Grad school was out of the question because I had not gotten a fellowship (for which I forced myself to apply). But when Mama offered to help me through grad school over the phone just before graduation, I jumped at it. I had been completely unsuccessful in trying to get a job, and I began to think that only by continuing my education would I be putting my time to good use. It is important, too, that at the time I accepted Mama's offer, studying intensely was far behind me. The last month and a half of college was a time of almost continuous loafing, and I felt very much like returning to studying. By the same token, I felt very cool toward grad school during the early spring, when I was writing my thesis and preparing for orals. Another strong incentive toward grad school was the urge to see another university and try my luck at getting good marks there. In a sense, then, I felt I would be missing out on something, I would not be taking full advantage of my training, if I did not go to grad school. There was no impelling drive, no certain goal—it is not because I want to teach or do literary criticism that I went to grad school, but because it seemed silly not to when the way was so easy.
>
> For roughly the same reason I went into German literature. At Harvard I was genuinely interested when I started out, but my interest tended to decrease rather than increase. Nevertheless, it was the field that I was most prepared to do successful graduate work in, and I certainly preferred literature to history. Now I feel a much greater urge to study English and American literature, but I doubt whether I would have been accepted as a graduate student in these fields anyway. It is likewise doubtful whether I would have been accepted as a comparative literature student at Harvard, which is of course the field I would have preferred. Columbia, on the other hand, did not have a comp. lit. department as such anyway. German was the only choice.

> I definitely preferred Columbia over Harvard even though I know the department here to be less astute, and the whole university much less so. To spend a year in the city was one of the main side ambitions of going to grad school. But I am somewhat disillusioned about all of it so far. The city has hardly been exciting, the work has been, as usual, monotonous and un-stimulating, and worst of all, I feel tired of and out of sorts with grad school altogether. My financial straits intensify this feeling, but they are not the cause. I simply do not enjoy this sort of thing, even though it comes fairly easily. The less work I have to do, the more I like it. The prospect of spending several more years at this purely mechanistic way of life is discouraging. And yet at a distance it had seemed so appealing, and probably will again. At this point it seems almost certain that I will not continue for a PhD.
>
> On the other hand, if I'm going to teach as a career, I would like to do so on as advanced a level as possible. If I teach in a secondary school, which I might not mind—although I certainly won't feel myself psychologically ready for that for several years—I would definitely want to teach history, or English—but not a language. Right now I lean more and more toward writing as a career, but I don't dare make a serious start of it.

Two weeks later the presidential election brought back memories of election eve at Harvard four years before. On 6 November 1956 I wrote an entry in my journal, which, though entirely self-absorbed, says something about the "strait-jacketed fifties" as well:

> Election day evening! What I remember most about election evening four years ago is my acute consciousness at the time that by the next presidential election I would be graduated from Harvard and well-launched on a career. It seemed a huge, hardly fathomable thought at the time. I remember thinking, yes, in four years I will be somewhere. And at the same time I thought, how short is the time and how aware one has to be of every moment in order to get the most out of it. I spent that evening in Sy's room, playing cards, drinking beer, doing nothing, and wishing and pretending I were doing something. A few things stick out—Sy disowning New Jersey [which went for Eisenhower], the burning of the Stevenson poster, Sy's Spanish exam in the morning, Vern and Paul Steveken for Ike. Sy put away his big Stevenson button for '56.

This seemed to me funny and absurd. '56 seemed like an inconceivable distance, not so much because of the time, but because so much had to transpire before then. How could one logically grasp the existence in the bureau drawer of the Stevenson button, quietly waiting, while four years at Harvard passed? One has the same feeling sometimes when one goes to bed before a big event the next day and simply cannot conceive of the same time tomorrow night when it would all be over. So much will have changed!

And how little actually has changed. Some education, a few more concepts, meeting Paul (probably the most important item)—but in the end the same listless, restive, frustrated feeling, only more so, because on a wider scale, and because older. Then I could find relief in the thought of being in the first year of college with so much more to come, with '56 as a glorious goal, even though not really enjoying the present. Now relief is not so readily available in thoughts of the future, and present activity. At that time I had never had a real "date," feeling insufficient and looking again to the next few years to correct this. Well, now where am I? I have met many girls, I can conduct myself easily with them, and I am conscious of being attractive enough. But still the same trouble: I felt myself attractive enough then too, but—and not despite it, but because of it—I felt incapable of "handling" a girl I liked, although I intensely desired it. I felt myself unable to carry out the expected things as expected. I am beyond the original stage now, but that same actual feeling is more deeply entrenched now. I have only kissed one girl, and that was in no way stimulating. I have felt incapable of kissing a girl, even though (or in fact because) she was expecting it, prepared for it, ready to enjoy it—that is the main reason for the Madge failure. And yet I can intensely desire to kiss a girl at the same time that I consciously decide I can't.

Four years later, then, I have the same trouble. I have the objective—Nancy and Nicki—and still that gnawing feeling of insufficiency. Not exactly that, though, because I know that I would suffice, if I could only bring myself to act. Inertia, it is, the more frustrating because of the over-zealous imagination which so urgently wants me to act. All it takes is an act of will, Paul said. True, but what does it take to take this act of will? I do so much better in unusual situations, when nothing is expected, when

> things are not "done" in a certain way. I can't get close to girls because I continually think of it as playing out a dating pattern. There is something delicious in having a date, because you are sure of her for a while, but also something crushing and stagnating because flirtation isn't possible, real inter-probing, penetration, because there are certain things one does, period. And I can't understand how a good-night kiss could ever be natural.
>
> My personality has not changed, though a few things have happened. The remedy was as clear then as now, and still I have not cured myself. All one has to fear is fear itself—this is true not only of politics. The line is pointed, but how to go about it? And so off to Betsy's.

One of the attractions of moving to New York was that my sister Betsy lived there, in an apartment on West 86th Street (later on W 87th), as I recall, and I often went to her place for supper. We would polish off a loaf of fresh-baked Jewish rye with honey before even sitting down to supper! Betsy was finishing her studies at Barnard, financing her education entirely on her own, as Mama refused to provide any support after her marriage to David Rothenberg. Unfortunately, their marriage was now breaking down. David moved out that fall and got a place of his own, although he maintained friendly relations both with Betsy and me. Both Betsy and David began dating other people, and it seemed only a question of time before they would get divorced. Yet I managed to keep on good terms with David, who at one point called me the closest male friend he had at that time. Perhaps that was because I often defended him to Betsy, not necessarily because I thought he was right, but because he needed defense so badly.

David was thoroughly disillusioned with marriage. "When you're married you're typed," he told me; "you become the Rothenbergs—a unit—you're not people anymore. Marriage is the most lonely institution." Then he compared his situation to mine:

> Life is really interesting. I never had a home, my parents never liked me—they told me that they would have had an abortion if it hadn't been too late, and that's why I'm a roamer, I have the option to pick and take whatever pleases me, and to reject and avoid what doesn't. I think you're kind of in the same boat. You had a home, but I think you were always kept at arm's length. We have no roots, no compulsion to do a

certain thing, nothing to fall back on. It can be both a handicap and an advantage.

Meanwhile, I was losing ever more interest in my studies, while at the same time indulging a hopeless infatuation with a pretty Italian-American girl by the name of Nicole (Nicki), who worked in the comptroller's office and delivered the monthly pay checks to the Columbia Business School, where I held a part-time job. Betsy made fun of me for my completely fantasized romance and sexual naiveté, and I was envious (and critical) of her for the very real nature of her romantic relationships. The most telling barb she directed at me (as recorded in my journal) was, "Live a little, Lodi! You'll learn something." That struck home. Here I was at Columbia graduate school with a Harvard degree and had never even had sex with a woman. In college, Paul and I were very aware that we were the last generation to be so "up-tight" (a term that would not enter the general vocabulary until the sixties) about sex. We very much regretted not living in an age in which sexual intercourse would become as routine as kissing a girl goodnight—an age we felt sure could not be far off.

Much of my social life in New York took place in the Lion's Den, the student lounge on the Columbia campus, where a diverse group of Betsy's friends gathered every day. More and more, however, as the semester wore on, the locus of our get-togethers shifted to the West End Bar on Broadway. This was the scene of some heavy drinking on my part over the course of the next few months as I recklessly plunged into "real life" after sixteen years of "book learning." One evening at about midnight the bartender paid me a dubious compliment: "We opened two barrels of beer tonight – one for you, and one for the rest of our customers." Trying to account for my excessive drinking in my journal, I blamed it on my hyper-nervousness, noting that "my stomach leaves me in perfect peace when I'm drunk." I did meet some interesting people there, including the Juillard student Albert Fine (1932-1987), to whom I gave my Beethoven paper to read at his request, but unfortunately I never got it back.

The effects of my dissipation soon became apparent in my academic performance and in my attitude toward school. In a journal entry on 3 January 1957 I tried to sort out my future plans:

My present turmoil is on what to do next term. Whether to ask Mama for

> money to finish, which I know she would provide—although it would be an immense chore to get it? I feel several conflicting sentiments. One, of course, to finish and make the year worth it, and be relatively secure. The other, to get completely away from studying, to work, make money, have an apartment, live better, have leisure. Lesser, but guiding sentiments: not to ask Mama, to, in effect, declare independence—despite the fact that I know to continue school would be safest, and most worthwhile not to leave Columbia, to pursue the Nicki disease to its end, rather than escape. To take Mark Van Doren's course. To try for the Information Service, which wants MA's. To be here in the spring. But I must face the fact that I hate to study, that I have not enjoyed any of my courses this fall, that I have befriended no professor, that I have not once visited Deutsches Haus, that I am, in fact, languishing and floating.
>
> On what criteria to decide? Mere personal preferences won't suffice, because they are ambiguous and nebulous. I don't know what I prefer, quite bluntly, and it is as much this as anything that I have to find out. It is not a question of deciding what is best for me, only insofar as it influences my wishes, desires, ambitions.

I also had an all-too-ready rationale for not pursuing what I claimed to be my strongest ambition:

> I have a loathing for the second-rate, the mediocre—that is one reason why I don't start writing seriously. Only when "second-ratism" is inherent in the thing to be done itself, and the very best execution cannot make it first-rate—as for instance the work at the Busy School, or any work I might get now—is it tolerable. Writing is intrinsically first-rate, it requires the finest in talent and skill.

And so I looked for a job, with no particular field in mind and no further aim than to make some money. Money alone was not the object, however. Otherwise I would have applied for one of the many executive trainee positions that filled the classified ads every day. But I knew that I didn't want to go into the corporate world as a career. On January 4th I wrote:

> Tomorrow I have an interview for a job, which was advertised in the *Saturday Review*. It is apparently a "remedial reading" teaching job, at different prep schools in the east. I was, of course, wary and unsure

> immediately on hearing that it was a teaching job, for which I feel myself so inadequate. But I've made up my mind to muster as much interest and enthusiasm for it as I can. As Mrs. Lister [a secretary at the Business School] said about her new job, it will do a lot of good even if nothing comes of it.

Two days later I wrote:

> My interview for a job went fairly well. The salary offered is low enough to give me a good chance. The fact that he gave me the only copy of the textbook to read and asked me to come back next week is encouraging. If I get it, I think I will do it. To tear myself away with spring coming is going to mean a few depressed, regretful hours. And to miss Mark Van Doren's poetry course too.

The job, in fact, was to teach "speed reading," a growing fashion that was destined to generate a lot of profits for proliferating self-styled "developmental reading firms" in the next decade or so. The most famous and financially successful of these would be Evelyn Woods's mass discount speed-reading program before it exhausted the market and faded away in the late 1960s. "Speed reading" caught the public mood in an expanding economy deluged by printed materials in the late 1950s, as schools and businesses sought to gain a competitive advantage by equipping their students and executives with time-saving skills. My employer, Ken Baldridge, then in his late 30s, was one of the pioneers of this field and had written the only existing textbook on how to increase one's reading speed without sacrificing comprehension. Ken was a dynamic entrepreneurial type who insisted with messianic fervor that improving reading skills was an essential key to a successful professional or business career. When I met him in early 1957 he was starting his own firm, Baldridge Reading Services. His idea was to offer six- to eight-week "developmental reading" courses by trained specialists at school sites using the latest technological devices, including mechanical "flashers" that would supposedly train students to read in phrases rather than word-by-word, and "reading pacers," screens that descended the page at adjustable speeds to force the reader to read faster. Ken envisioned a time when a certificate of having completed such a course would become a prerequisite for college admission. His program was aimed toward private college preparatory schools, the only secondary schools with a clientele that could afford the rather expensive rate of $100 per student for the 30-hour course. Classes were to be kept small to ensure individual attention. I was to become Ken's first employee in a business destined to grow rapidly over the next several months. As an Ivy League graduate with an east-coast accent (which earned me Ken's sobriquet, "the voice"), I fulfilled the major qualifications Ken was looking for. My skepticism about the need for or value of "speed reading" was no impediment at all. I soon discovered that we could safely guarantee to double a student's reading speed. Making a conscious effort to read as fast as one can is all that is required to enable average readers to significantly increase their reading rates. The only real challenge we faced was to convert such deliberate effort into a lasting habit. In that sense the courses we offered were part of a widespread trend toward the kind of motivational training that came into its own in the economic boom years of the late 1950s and the 1960s.

Ken started his business with his young wife Dusty from his home in Ossining, NY, a few miles north of the city, although he used a Pleasantville address on his business letterhead, perhaps because Ossining was too well known as the home of the notorious Sing Sing penitentiary. Later that spring he acquired an old residential building at 47 Arch Street in Greenwich, Connecticut, and converted it into the Baldridge Reading Services business office. Meanwhile, my Harvard classmate Dick Shader, who was attending medical school at NYU, invited me to share his two-room apartment on Charles Street in Greenwich Village while I was in New York between my private school assignments. This enabled me to avoid rush-hour traffic by reversing the usual commuting pattern: rather than driving from the suburbs to work in the city as most people did, I had an easy drive in the northbound lanes from the city to my work in Greenwich and an equally easy return to the city in the afternoon. That spring I bought my first real car. I had briefly owned a miniature Crosley with a 2-cycled engine in college. It had died on the road on my way home for Thanksgiving vacation in 1954 when a piston rammed through the cylinder head with a terrifying bang. The car that I bought in 1957 was a fairly late-model Oldsmobile, but with around 100,000 miles, most of them put on by the dishonest dealer from whom I bought the car. The carburetor needed repeated repairs. Dick Shader expressed puzzlement at my recurring mechanical troubles. "Humans are unreliable and unpredictable," he said; "machines are not." This seemed like a revelation to me. "Mechanically challenged" as I was (in today's lingo), I had always thought of machines as inherently unreliable. The notion that with proper care and attention they could actually be more dependable than people was a novelty to me.

Dick Shader also introduced me to the guitar, which I learned well enough to accompany the folk songs that I picked up from Weavers records or Pete Seeger's well-worn print collections. Folk-singing was the typical mode of expression of mildly alienated youth in the conformist 1950s, combining a yearning for authenticity with a sense of community (the appeal of the sing-along) and an unabashed sentimentality with mostly unfocused social protest. It was not yet the personal, political, and highly creative art form that it was to become under the influence of Bob Dylan and the social liberation movements of the 1960s. It did not occur to me that I should at least try to write my own songs. That would presume that I could improve on the standards and traditions of the past.

My first assignment as a "developmental reading" instructor was at St. George's School in Newport, Rhode Island, in April and May 1957. Because Ken had so many contract proposals to prospective client schools to complete, we didn't leave Ossining until about midnight, driving through the night and getting about two hours of sleep at a motel in Newport before meeting our appointment for breakfast with the headmaster at 8 a.m. The developmental reading course at St. George's was a great success. The work was easy, students and faculty were congenial, and my living quarters in one of the dorms were comfortable and private. One of the teachers at St. George's, Chip Ludlow, who went on to a long career at Kent School (where he became one of my daughter's teachers in the 1980s), told me he would not want to trade places with me, because by spending only six to eight weeks at any one school I never got to see my students develop over the years, but this lack of real responsibility for their intellectual growth was one of the attractions of my job for me at the time. My favorite activity after classes was to ogle the mansions on Ocean Drive, especially one that was open to the elements and in disrepair, with all the furnishings still in place from the time it had been abandoned many years earlier. I used the weekends to visit Paul and Sy in Boston or to meet up with Tempy, who was completing his freshman year at UConn. What I did not do was use my plentiful leisure hours in any literarily productive way, despite my intention to start some serious writing that spring.

Teaching speed-reading at St. George's School, spring 1957

There was even more time to waste on my second assignment, at Germantown Academy in Philadelphia in June and July 1957. I had only two morning classes and the rest of the day to myself. Ken had asked me to write a training manual for the rapidly growing number of new Reading Services instructors in my extra time, but this took only a minimum of effort. The rest of the time I lay, naked and sweating, on my bed on one of the top floors of the YMCA building where I was housed, listening to music or baseball games on the radio. The heat in July was intense, and the highlight of my day was to have supper in an air-conditioned cafeteria. I also did a lot of walking through the city, hitting all the historic Philadelphia landmarks. An entry in my journal on the 4th of July expressed my mood at the time:

> My life in Germantown has been a do-nothing one, and yet I've enjoyed it. I like being able to loaf. One gets sick of loafing, but one gets sicker if one doesn't have the privilege of choosing to loaf. Of course, I'm dissatisfied that I don't have interesting things to do, people to see, but one can live happily for a long time in a world where things are "possible". In a very disciplined kind of life there are no such possibilities. Much of the pleasure I currently get out of life is anticipating—and dreaming—but it is pleasure, nevertheless.

On weekends I always returned to New York, but I didn't put my time to any better use. Here is my entry on a day at the beach on June 13th:

> Spent the afternoon and evening alone at Coney Island, doing nothing but looking, and eating disgusting food. I had a long conversation with a drunk , a Joe Ryan from Boston. I mentioned I had been in Boston, and he asked if I had gone to Harvard. "You look like a Harvard man, but you need a shave." He was perfectly aware of his alcoholism. He brandished an A.A. card, citing his intention to sit in on a session that very evening. Like most drunks he was extremely friendly, voluble, with a strong leaning toward humor, very much like Danny [Ashman]: a "life is just a bowl of cherries" attitude which his very actions—his drunkenness—denied. He had a little money from his mother, and he was extremely generous with it, tipping a shoe-shine boy heavily and giving it to urchins. I tried to sound him out on why he drank. He was only 38, but looked like 48, with grey hair. He had been married in 1942 to a grand-niece of a cardinal. He was divorced in '49. He showed me the pictures of his two daughters. His brothers were "upstanding" and successful. A man like that will do anything for his liquor; he is weak as a child and pliable and pathetic.

One place I rarely went that summer or fall was home to Canaan. I did feel guilty when I heard that Tempy had assured Mama that I was coming on a particular weekend because I had said I would: "If he said he will come, he will come." My guilt was for undermining Tempy's trust in my word. He unintentionally paid me back in kind that fall when I drove from Newport (where I was doing a second six-week stint at St. George's) to Storrs to surprise him one Saturday only to find that he had left for Canaan shortly before. Mama said that Tempy had been strongly affected by the breakup of our family when all of his siblings went their separate ways. Olaf was now in the army, stationed at the biological warfare lab at Fort Detrick in Frederick, Maryland, where I visited him in the spring of 1958, shortly after the birth of his first son, John.

John Sleighter Stackelberg, 1959

Mama asked me to talk to Tempy to try to get him to take his studies more seriously. Apparently she was unaware (or was she?) that I was the wrong person to give any advice on how to put one's nose to the grindstone! I dutifully lectured him, coming away only with the feeling of being a sanctimonious hypocrite and a royal pain in the neck. In February 1958 Mama decided to send Tempy to Germany to continue his education there. She wrote to Papa, who offered to pay for his trip and his stay.

That year, 1957 to 1958, I formed a strong attachment to Carole Seversen, recently hired as a co-worker at Baldridge Reading Services (BRS). Carole was under some pressure from her mother to get married, as were many young women at that time. Ken later told me that when he first interviewed her she said she'd gone to a coed college, but "nothing happened." I was not in the least bit ready to get married. This was a function of my own personal immaturity, but also a reflection of the pre-feminist culture of the 1950s, which extolled marriage and child-rearing for young women and thus provided, at least indirectly, an inducement for young men to try to escape the ever-threatening (but always available) "marriage trap" (well-captured in Updike's *Run, Rabbit, Run*). Although it was rarely openly acknowledged, the sexual prudery of the 1950s also bred a subculture among young males that esteemed bedding as many women as possible without getting "trapped." In college we regarded with considerable awe and envy (and some incredulity) those of our classmates who notched sexual conquests without taking on any reciprocal obligations. Paul, Sy, and I actually made a pact to buy dinner for the first of us who lost his virginity (without cheating, i.e., without the services of a prostitute), although none of us ever claimed the prize, and it remained a mystery who of us won that particular contest.

Eventually I paid the price for my refusal to make more than an emotional commitment to my relationship with Carole. In Los Angeles, where I had gone to open a California office for BRS in April 1958, hoping and expecting that Carole would eventually follow, I received a "Dear John" letter informing me of her forthcoming marriage to a former boy friend she had been stringing along for several years. She also left me in no doubt that nothing I could now do would change her mind (although I was strongly tempted for weeks, even months, to put that postulate to the test). Not for the last time in my life the moment of loss became the moment of truth. Writing about the experience in my journal helped me to overcome the pain:

> On my 23rd birthday [8 May1958], a brief review of the Carole episode, which in the past two weeks has robbed me of all serenity: she had early become stereotyped in my mind as a girl I would "play" with, but never marry. During the past eight months we have gone through many phases of intimate courtship together, and most of the time I had the feeling, "God, this is fun, but how I wish it was 'for real'." That it could be 'for real' never once seriously occurred to me. And I heeded none of the danger signs: the fact that I missed her inordinately, the fact that I invariably enjoyed being with her. Toward the end, as it now appears in retrospect, this stereotype of a girl at my beck and call whom I would not want to marry, had stuck so fast, that I was completely oblivious to the fact that I had fallen in love. My whole last week and a half in Greenwich was scheduled around Carole, so to speak; I tried to see her at every possible

> opportunity, I dreaded any activity that took me away from her—and yet I never faced the apparent fact that I loved her very much. This then was one of those affairs where the torture comes later, the torture of chances missed. In the beginning I had decided she was not the girl for me, a) because I was not strongly attracted to her physically, b) because of her provincial, small-town, sorority girl talk and ways. In the end there was no girl to whom I felt more attracted physically, whom I would rather kiss or sleep with; or whose affectionate ways and voluble small talk about this and that, but mostly nothing, were more lovable or dearer to me. But I was blind to it. I just took it and enjoyed myself and warmed myself on her, and gave never a thought to the future. I took her too much for granted, and while I was enjoying her most I lost her, and I didn't realize that either, until it was too late.

Ken, who of course saw the relationship from an entirely different vantage point, later annoyed me by attributing my infatuation to "the desire for a mate, and Carole was the nearest object." But my annoyance probably stemmed from the truth of this remark, and also of his well-meaning admonition: "In marriage nothing can be contrived. All the façades come down."

The desultory dissipation that had begun while I was still at Columbia but grew worse in the course of 1957 (though limited to occasional heavy drinking and smoking cigarettes) eventually took its toll on my health. In January 1958, after spending a couple of nights in the damp unfinished basement at 47 Arch Street in Greenwich rather than returning to the city (thus gaining a couple of hours that would otherwise have been spent driving back and forth), I came down with the flu, which rapidly turned to life-threatening pneumonia. I remember my disappointment at having to turn down Dick Shader's invitation to join him on a blind double date with all its hidden promise. It remained in my imagination one of those turning points when my life might have taken an entirely different turn, if fate had not arbitrarily intervened. Instead I ended up in the hospital in Ossining for two weeks. On the phone Mama asked my physician point blank whether I was going to die, but he would only say that I hadn't yet responded to medication. When Olaf called Mama on her birthday, January 20th, to report that his son John had been born that same day, he was stunned to hear from her that I was "in the hospital dying." Although I felt very sick, I was not aware of how serious my condition was, and the thought that I might die never entered my mind. Only later did I realize that I had been given a wholly unmerited second chance at life. Betsy, Uncle Nick, and my first cousin Ginny Biddle came to visit me in the hospital. The Baldridges greatly assisted in my recovery by welcoming me into their home after my hospital stay and by continuing to pay my weekly salary even when I was unable to work, which they were under no legal obligation to do. Mama told me the Biddles were quite impressed that I was so well-liked by my employers. I had no health insurance, of course, but because of the free room and board I was able to pay off the entire $800 hospital bill before the end of my next school assignment, at Wyoming Seminary in Kingston, Pennsylvania, in February and March of that year.

In early April I left the east coast for California to open a Los Angeles office for our expanding firm. My last phone call to Mama left me reassured that things were going as usual on the farm. She certainly hadn't lost her sense of humor, as recorded in my journal:

> Mama has a new hired man—"the shouter." He shouts at the cows and lives in the little house, which to him is a castle despite no toilet and no water. "He's never had them anyway." He wages an unending battle against the manure, but he doesn't like it. It's "too shitty."

Mama, who had never been west of the Mississippi, said she would love to accompany me just to see the west (her father was born in Prescott, AZ, and her grandfather had been a career officer stationed mostly in Indian country in Wyoming), but of course she could not get away. I left Greenwich early in the morning in a state of youthful euphoria, intending to drive the entire way. My Oldsmobile did not let me down . Driving sixteen to eighteen hours a day, and sleeping in my car by the side of the road in those pre-interstate days, I reached Phoenix, AZ, via venerable Route 66 in the early afternoon on the fourth day. Here I had an appointment to try to sell our reading program to the head of a private school, before proceeding on to LA and a new phase of my life the following day.

6
The Army, 1958-1960

In Los Angeles I rented a house with three other young men at 1109 Longwood Avenue and set about establishing a small business office for Baldridge Reading Services (BRS) in a spanking new office building on Wilshire Boulevard. The office was too small to conduct classes, but I did offer individual after-school instruction. The only student I still remember was the son of the Hollywood star Wendell Corey (1914-1968). He came to the office one day to inquire about the progress of his son. By that time the reassuring phrases we were trained to offer had become so second-nature to me that I had no trouble at all maintaining a calm professional demeanor. My main task in Los Angeles was to try to sell our reading program to prospective clients, the heads of the private college preparatory schools in California. At this task I was pretty good. Although at times I got a quick brush-off, in general the many secondary school (and some college) educators I talked to seemed to like me, which, I eventually concluded, was the key to successful salesmanship. Teaching (at least on the secondary or undergraduate level) and selling, I thought, had at least one characteristic in common in that in both vocations likeability played a central role in success. Of course, success is more likely when one has a popular and useful product to sell (or subject to teach), but in my experience at least, popularity (and hence success in the classroom or in closing a deal) was more a function of personality than of any specific trainable skill. I summed up the relationship between teaching and selling in a rather cynical journal entry:

"Developmental reading" as auto-suggestion: successive stages of

> persuasion: first you persuade them they need to read fast, then you persuade them they're learning how to read fast, then you persuade them they've learned to read fast. Make 'em like it and they won't notice what's happened. Whether anything has actually been accomplished is secondary to whether the student thinks something's been accomplished. Questionnaires are most blatant examples of auto-suggestive gimmicks. Techniques employed are those of salesman: advantages first: serve everything up wrapped in an advantage.

Evidently, my heart was not in my work. I looked forward to the evenings when I could goof off with my new-found friends, as unfulfilling as our nightly outings might turn out to be. We partied a lot and often went to the beach after work, usually in Santa Monica. One weekend we took a day trip to Tijuana right across the Mexican border. I was surprised to see a dead dog lying on the sidewalk as if it were the most normal thing in the world. My friends were always in search of beddable girls. I consoled myself for my ineptitude in that particular competition by telling myself that my standards were much higher than theirs. Nothing could fill the void left by my break-up with Carole, which occurred by mail a few weeks into my California sojourn. My most intense memory of those days is the desperate loneliness I felt on one of my sales trips to the San Francisco area when I spent the night in my car and woke up wondering what on earth had brought me to this particular station of life. Already at Wyoming Seminary I had confided to my journal

> my growing conviction that this job and way of life must have a *raison d'être*, that if I do not find it, I should give up the job. The work itself, though interesting and gratifying at times, is not sufficient *raison d'être* in itself. The two foremost ones (and they have been since I began): leisure and privacy and freedom to write; and the opportunity to save a lot of money, for an, at this time, indeterminate purpose. Since I have not yet begun to write—even at Germantown where I had all day and the whole city—I hardly expect to produce anything here. Time and leisure may be present, but there is something about these school settings—perhaps, the stultifying routine, or the un-homelike atmosphere (friendly and congenial though it may be) that freezes initiative and nurtures lethargy. My big consolation is that I have never yet made a real effort. It is wrong to think, as I have, that one must wait for the spirit to strike. It is true

> that most of my "insights," such as they are, have "come" at unexpected times, generally either when pencil and paper were not handy or when there was no chance to use them. But insights are more abundant and generally clearer when "sought out" by dint of hard work.

But nothing changed in California—and here I could not blame my inertia on stultifying school settings. Potential deliverance from my quandary came rather suddenly and unexpectedly in the form of a notice from my draft board in Torrington, Connecticut, to report for induction into the army in July.

For this reason, but possibly also because he sensed my irresolution, Ken Baldridge decided to send a replacement for me to California and assigned me instead to conduct a six-week reading program at the Pembroke-Country Day School in Kansas City. Here on 14 June 1958 I recorded some further reflections about my future, which turned out to be quite perspicacious for a change:

> This may well be the last program I take. July 15 [later postponed until August 9th] I am scheduled for induction, and even if I should be rejected, I'm determined to make a change as soon as possible. The prospect of another two month spell at St. George's is most distasteful. I am fitted for university teaching, and that's what I'm going to do. This endless travel in the end becomes absurd. And though the temptation to stay with BRS, because it is growing, because it has interesting, congenial members, because it will be prosperous,—though the temptation is very strong, I do not think I will succumb. If I go into the army I may very well return for a spell after coming out, just to meet the new people and the old people, earn some money, get back into something I know how to do well. But not for long—unless, of course, Ken apprehends this feeling and makes it very much worth my while to stay. He undoubtedly realizes by now that I'm as un-title-conscious as it is possible to be, almost to a fault. I don't think he realized this last summer when he made an apologetic call to Philadelphia to explain that Dave Brown was being called "assistant to the director"—"for promotion purposes." He went on to assure me that it meant nothing. Of course it meant something, but Ken didn't realize until recently that he didn't need to assuage me. I just didn't care that much. This, of course, gives him more cause for worry than if I took titles very

> seriously, at least if he wants me to stay, because it means that I don't regard this as my life's work, to say the very least.

Ken did indeed apprehend my ambivalence, and he made a special trip to Kansas City to persuade me to do everything I could to stay out of the army. On 17 July 1958 I recorded his visit in my journal:

> He came very softly, carrying a frisbee, and he caught me somewhat by surprise. Almost the first thing he said: "We've got to keep you out of the army—that's why I'm here. We've got lots of incentives for you: 100 dollars a week starting Sept. 30, a bonus for every sale you make, $7,200 a year within four years, head of a center in Boston, near the Cliffdwellers. Call Midge [Oberheim] and ask her to come in for a Refresher session. You can have anything you want."

In the two weeks before my scheduled induction I took a whirlwind two-week sales trip through the South, meeting appointments that had been made for me at the BRS headquarters in Greenwich. The trip, though successful enough in terms of signing up new clients for our reading program, did not do anything to make me happier with my job. An entry in my journal on July 29th gave expression not only to my ennui, but also to a complacency that, in retrospect, can too easily be blamed on the political quietism of the times:

> A trip of pure "move" like Ken's pure "drive." No satisfaction in visiting a place except the somewhat manufactured feeling, "I am now in Savannah, Georgia." Every once in a while I will remember, oh, I ought to look at the countryside; after all this is Texas, of TV cowboy fame, or Alabama, land o'cotton (I had to ask a hitchhiker what cotton plants look like, found out I had seen some, determined to enjoy it the next time I saw some). When I remember, which is infrequently, I scan the country-side in the vain hope of being thrilled. Not that there isn't much to be seen: but here the anticipation somehow eclipses the actuality, and actual sights pale in the light of colorful pre-imaginings. True also, to an extent, of local customs, peculiarities. For instance, segregation: this in theory has always struck me as an impossible system, against the grain, promoting continual tension, stamping in some perpetually noticeable way the entire Southern way of life. In actuality, I had forgotten completely about segregation until I saw a discreet window sign in a rural restaurant, "all-white." It's only from the outside, after all, that these things appear unusual, and one quickly

> settles into the prevailing frame of mind, where segregation is simply a long-standing way of life, like having dinner at 8.

That there were many courageous activists already battling the system in the fifties and that I might have joined in their protest never entered my mind at the time. My underdeveloped political consciousness may also have contributed to my failure to make any effort to avoid the draft and stay out of the army. I did indeed have the chance. X-rays taken at my physical examination had revealed scars from my recent near-fatal bout of pneumonia. I was commandeered out of the line of naked inductees and told to report to a board of military physicians, with whom the final decision rested. Here I was asked, "Are you sure you'll be able to hack it?" I had every chance to exaggerate my pulmonary infirmity, knowing that the army would not wish to be saddled with a potential medical liability. But perversely I only felt the need to repudiate the implication that I didn't have what it takes to endure the physical challenges of military service.

I have often wondered what my reaction would have been had the United States already been heavily involved in the Vietnam War. But this was not yet the case, even though during basic training in August and September 1958 our drill sergeant seemed to know what was coming when he threatened, "You'se guys is all gonna see combat in Viet Nam." Few of the recruits had ever heard of the place. I, for one, still believed the official propaganda that the Vietnamese were fighting for the liberation of their country from communism. Even though it soon became clear to me that I had indeed been drafted into an army preparing for war, it was still a time of peace. The Korean War had ended five years before, and in 1958 the tedium and vapidity of army life were greater deterrents to military service than the danger of risking one's life. On November 1st I recorded my reflections on eight weeks of basic training at Fort Leonard Wood in the Ozark Mountains in southern Missouri, reputed to be the grimmest army post in the country:

> What I remember now is lots of sweat, a chronic fatigue, a voracious appetite, constipation—the result of loss of privacy—never any time, always a whiplash shout, a dirty word—and the relentless momentum of time, from break to break to break to break, from chow to chow to chow, from mail-call to mail-call, from Saturday noon to Saturday noon.
>
> And in it all I remember certain moments of serenity, of absolute calm,

as if everything stood still, all except a cleansing breeze. These moments were the sources of greatest enjoyment, or more accurately contentment, during basic. Those were moments I've already ceased to have, that perhaps go entirely unnoticed in normal life. For in a serene life it is the turbulent that sticks out and generally gives the greatest pleasure. But in a hectic life it is the serene that becomes most pleasurable, or more accurately, most satisfying.

Then I went on leave and felt in a calm, secure way very good. I must confess, abashedly, to pride in the uniform. Also, I felt no inner qualms, none of those little tortures that used to harass my pre-military life. I had that small sense of belonging that gives every soldier his strength. From Reading Services, by all odds a better job, a better life, I never got it. The fact that I was drafted, that it was not by choice that I'm a soldier, actually contributed to my "mental well-being." No one could call me to task, and even I couldn't call myself to task for my present life. This is the consolation for doing something one has to. It's a great relief to put the super-ego and the whole will-mechanism to bed for a while. That, of course, is the popular rationalization for army duty, "it'll give me time to think."

Basic training is "hard," not because of any physical demands, but because of the massive humiliation. By the same token army life is "easy," not because duties are easy, but because there is no need, no sense to drive oneself. The army takes care of its own, it tells them what to do, when to do it, etc., etc. And except for the limited area of his immediate duties, the ordinary soldier has no large responsibility, just small, predictable ones. And, most important, he has no sense of guilt, none of that nagging obligation to self that characterizes civilian life with its immense freedom. The army limits and narrows the horizon, and the soldier has that happy, secure feeling that an animal might have in a well-provided zoo, safe from the struggle for survival without. And like the confined animal, the soldier, while enjoying the safety that those symbolic fences provide, will yearn to be outside. But the only real qualm he will feel is that he's wasting his time. For the younger ones there is always sufficient false adventure on the edges of army life to make them happy. But for the older ones, for the great body of draftees, army life represents a suspension, only too often a very welcome suspension, of large-scale choice and large-scale decision.

I also had time to reflect on some of these larger issues.

> The many obstacles that confront an attempt to evolve a "meaningful life"—and all of the concrete decisions depending on that concept, such as "what career shall I pursue?" or "which girl shall I marry?"—can for me be included under one highly inadequate heading: the arbitrariness of life. Perhaps this is just a prolix way of saying the obvious: the reason it is so hard to evolve a meaningful life is that life seems to have no meaning, no easily recognizable one, at least!

A week later, on November 17th, I thought I could give an example of the "arbitrariness of life" from the "clerk-typist" training I was then undergoing at Ft. Leonard Wood:

> Our squad leaders here were chosen on one criterion only: solely by height! But I thoroughly approve, and not because they are either good or bad. I thoroughly approve because of the extraordinary, the self-condemning absurdity of choosing squad leaders solely because they are tall. Nothing can so effectively give the lie to the whole system. In basic training, the arbitrariness of the squad leaders' selection was hypocritically cloaked behind protestations that superior qualities of "leadership" led to their choice. Here the arbitrariness is in no way denied. And shorter aspirants may find comfort in the reflection that the only reason they are not squad leaders is that they do not have the requisite height. Moreover, the tall ones are put on their mettle. Their "elevated" status—a pun is hard to resist—is due simply to the pituitary gland. What's more, they have so far proven quite excellent. The danger of arbitrariness is when it's hypocritically concealed, falsely rationalized—and mostly it is.

I derived benefits from the arbitrariness of the system myself. Most clerk-typist trainees, if they were draftees as the vast majority were, had no control at all to which branch of the army they would eventually be assigned or where they would be stationed. However, as an incentive to do well, we were told that the top three scorers on the standardized exam given at the end of clerk-typist training would be asked to what part of the United States or the world they wished to be posted. If there were suitable openings in these areas, their wishes would be heeded. Thus it happened that I became the only one in my unit to be posted to Germany, my first choice. I was so delighted by this news that I asked the top sergeant in the office responsible for issuing these orders what I could do for him. He said that a fifth of whiskey would always be appreciated. My return to Germany was to be as a clerk-typist in the Chemical Division of the U. S. Army, Europe (USAREUR) headquarters in picturesque Heidelberg, as desirable a posting as I could have wished. Our main tasks would be to map the area of radioactive fallout and estimate the number of civilian casualties from the use of battlefield nuclear weapons—and this at a time when the U.S. Government denied that there were any nuclear weapons stockpiled in Europe. The official policy under the Eisenhower administration remained "massive retaliation." For this sensitive assignment I needed a top-secret security clearance. Only two years earlier Olaf had been denied a similar clearance because we had so many foreign relatives. My job interview at Harvard with a representative of the CIA had been cut short when I told him that my father was German. The ease with which I now received the necessary top-secret clearance reflected the enhanced status of the Federal Republic of Germany in the Western alliance after its remilitarization and integration into NATO in 1956.

Before leaving for Germany in early January 1959, I took two weeks' leave over Christmas to visit my mother and sister back east. From Olaf, now back in Minneapolis to complete his PhD in math after his discharge from the army, I had heard that Mama had been forced to leave her beloved Canaan farm in June 1958, while I was still in California. I found her now living in a run-down shack on the Conklin dairy farm on Rt. 82 in Amenia, New York, for which she paid $5 a month in rent. She shared her shack with the farm's main hired hand, Jimmy, whom she hoped to persuade to join her in operating a farm on the property she had purchased, with help in the form of a down payment from her niece Ginny Biddle, in the "Northeast Kingdom" of northern Vermont. Mama kept a few cows of her own on the Conklin farm, where she also helped with the milking, hoping to save enough money for the eventual move to the north. Despite her recent travails, which she blamed on the intervention of her relatives, however well-intentioned they might have been, Mama was full of enthusiasm, looking forward to her next adventure in life. Our attempt to visit her Vermont property failed, however, when my Oldsmobile, worn out by my extensive travels, conked out just as we were beginning our trip to the north. We were forced to stay in Amenia, where I read Pasternak's *Dr. Zhivago*, finishing the book at 4 a.m. the next morning. One of Pasternak's similes stuck in my mind because it seemed like a warning directed at me: consciousness is like the headlight on a locomotive. When beamed ahead it illuminates the way; when reflected back it blinds the engineer and makes him unable to function.

I also visited Betsy in New York, now married to her second husband, Gail Chandler (1932-2009), and expecting her twins, Christopher and Julie, born in February 1959. This marriage did not last much longer than her first one. Fearing Gail's violent temper after several episodes of domestic strife, Betsy would seek refuge with her children at Aunt Temple's in Andover, Massachusetts, in 1961.

Betsy's twins, Julie and Chris Chandler, 1960

And so I returned to Germany with the U.S. Army in early January 1959, twelve-and-a-half years after our departure in June 1946. Because I was posted to USAREUR headquarters, I had the good fortune of travelling by air, to which in those days the subaltern ranks were not usually entitled. The twelve-hour flight to the Rhein-Main air base in Frankfurt by military aircraft was for me one of suppressed excitement, but also of nervous anticipation at the prospect of meeting and getting to know my father, with whom I had had no contact of any kind since 1946. For some reason he never wrote to his children in America. Despite Tempy's mediation, it took me several days to "psyche" myself up to give Papa a call. I had no idea whether he (or his second wife) would welcome, or perhaps (even if only privately) resent, this second intrusion (after Tempy's a year before) into Papa's new family and his present life. One way or another, my arrival seemed bound to cause a disruption which I was very hesitant to inflict upon him or on Halinka. After several hard years immediately after the war, Papa had succeeded in making a lustrous career as one of originally only twelve lawyers authorized to litigate cases before the *Bundesgerichtshof*, Germany's highest court for civil and criminal appeals, and the *Verfassungsgericht*, the supreme court for constitutional cases, both located in the city of Karlsruhe (only 40 miles from Heidelberg on the Autobahn) in the southwestern state of Baden-Württemberg. The minimum age for lawyers to litigate cases at the *Bundesgericht* was 40 at the time, exactly my father's age. His admission to this select group in 1950, shortly after the founding of the *Bundesgerichtshof* in October 1949 (the Constitutional Court was established in 1951), was (at least in part) because he was one of relatively few German lawyers of his generation to emerge from the Nazi era entirely untainted by any Party affiliation. In the follow-up trials at Nuremberg he had been retained as a lawyer for the defense of, among others, the notorious Wilhelm Stuckart (1902-1953), the leading civil servant in the Interior Ministry under Wilhelm Frick (who was executed in October 1946 for crimes against humanity), but Papa's acceptance of this distasteful brief in no way signified any sympathy for Nazi ideology or any approval of Stuckart's shameful role in promoting and enforcing Nazi racial laws. However, the defense team of which Papa was a part was able to get Stuckart's sentence reduced to a minimal four years by invoking the legal principle of *nulla poena sine lege* (no punishment without law), arguing that Stuckart had broken no laws in effect at the time.

By the end of the 1950s, when I got to know Papa, he had become quite prosperous and corpulent, a beneficiary of the *Wirtschaftswunder* that began with the currency reform in 1948 and continued unabated throughout the next decade, as West Germany was integrated into the Western alliance. His experience of the Nazi era had left him quite disillusioned with politics and unwilling to commit himself to any political party, although he probably voted for the liberal (in the European sense of *laissez-faire*) Free Democratic

Party, whom he also represented in cases before the court. A cautious conservative, he felt very much at home in the new Federal Republic. More than once he remarked how terrible it would have been for the whole world, had Germany won the war. But he had not joined the military resistance, although invited to do so, giving the rather lame-sounding excuse that he could not be expected to violate his military oath. By the time I got to know him he was a formidable, and to me rather intimidating, personality, basking in professional and financial success. He was a *Lebenskünstler*, a *bon vivant* who understood how to lead the good life and could afford to do so. He sought to preserve, or recover, some of the time-honored customs of the Baltic aristocracy, including the delightful pre-dinner ritual of vodka and anchovy "sakuska." An excellent conversationalist and story-teller, with a good sense of humor and a gift for extemporaneous public speaking, he distrusted intensity and had little patience for overly serious people or for a tragic view of life. Over-awed by his grand seigneurial aura and his charm, I recorded my first reactions to the festive dinners over which he presided:

> Papa is the opposite of the Kafka-Kierkegaard type of personality, and oh what a wonderful opposite. His answer to those unspeakable problems of life, and I cannot believe that Papa is not aware of them, is to consciously—and I think his asthma is proof of his consciousness—get the most pleasures that life has to offer. When facing an enormous meal, with a couple of bottles of *Schnaps*, surrounded by congenial people, then all of Kafka's doubts and problematizing and tragedizing seem to be awfully far away, even irrelevant. The humorous approach to otherwise solemn topics is also an answer, very decidedly an answer, feasting as it does on the incongruities in reality. Papa has neat little compromises to the Big Questions—he doesn't believe too deeply in religion—that would take too much out of him—nor does he cut it down—he accepts it and even gets some satisfaction and, as he says, strength out of going to church [where he very often fell asleep]. If there were no such thing as religion, there'd probably be something else, but it wouldn't make any difference one way or another to Papa. Papa is aloof from politics. The state is there to keep law and order and let everybody live as they want to. He's the opposite of a fanatic, he's not about to die for or against anything. It is not hard to see how he would simply, perforce, go along with the Nazi regime: to be *unmittelbar* (unconditionally) against is not much different from being

> *unmittelbar* for. And his work, though in instances it no doubt interests him, even arouses him, is most important to him for the position, the influence, the *Ansehen* it guarantees him, for the respect and admiration, well-earned and richly deserved, that fall to him as a result, and, last but not least, because it allows him to live luxuriously.

Halinka was the perfect wife for him, waiting hand and foot on his every need or wish. She ran his bath for him every morning and laid out the shirt and the suit he was to wear that day. When occasionally she complained about his extravagance and generosity (spending money that she thought should more properly go to her own children), he responded to her censure with conciliatory irony. "*Ich versuche doch nur das Leben etwas erträglicher zu gestalten*" (I am only trying to make life a little more bearable), he would say, or something to that effect. They called each other "Süsses" (sweetheart) or "Mammilein" and "Pappilein" and genuinely enjoyed each other's company. I could not even imagine my mother as his wife.

Weekend feasts in Karlsruhe and the periodic balls and banquets put on by the regional organizations of the Baltic nobility, in which Papa played a leading role, counterbalanced the humdrum routine of army life. But I never felt entirely comfortable at these functions, always aware that I was after all an interloper from another time and another world. Despite the tutelage of my half-sisters, I never properly learned the intricate steps of the traditional Baltic dances. Although trained as a child to proffer the *Handkuss* to ladies, the gesture seemed anachronistic and unnatural to me now, and I cringed at the prospect of having to perform a ritual for which I had no feeling at all. Yet I didn't want to let my father down, to whom such social rituals were quite important and came very naturally. Consequently, I always felt like a bit of an impostor, unable to fulfill the expectations that my paternal ancestry seemed to impose on me. Knowing that Papa wanted nothing so much as to be proud of his sons and daughters, I felt very strongly my inability to gratify his wishes in this regard. My chosen role in the family was as a passive outsider. My foremost rule was to avoid any action that might upset the delicate family equilibrium or incur Papa's displeasure. Much as I enjoyed these elaborate family feasts, I never felt as if I was truly a part of the family.

More and more my social life consisted in drinking and hanging out with my new-found army buddies, most of them college-educated draftees, a group that was overrepresented at USAREUR headquarters. We led a life of unavoidable hypocrisy, forced day after day to keep saying and doing things in which we did not believe. We shared a generalized resentment against the disruption in our lives of army service, the pettiness of army rules, and the "chicken-shit" to which we were subjected at the bottom of the military hierarchy. We counted the days until our two-year terms of service would end. FTA (fuck the army) was our watchword. We engaged in small and relatively safe acts of defiance, such as deliberately altering our paths to avoid having to salute an officer heading our way. We nursed a barely concealed contempt for the "lifers" who took the army so seriously, the "truckers" who had volunteered for service or had reenlisted, and the MPs who, we felt, viewed us not as their allies against "the enemy," but as the enemy itself. In principle we approved of the notion of a "citizen army," disapproving only of the fact that we "citizens" had so little to say. The full potential of a citizen army was eventually revealed in Vietnam, where strife between "lifers" and draftees rose to unprecedented levels and frequent small-scale mutinies and "combat refusals" would eventually force the government to end that unjust war. No wonder that in 1973 the Nixon Administration ended the draft and created the All-Volunteer Force—in reality a professional army purged of dissent and refusal, the precondition for the "new American militarism" (the title of a recent book by historian Andrew Bacevich) that has continued to dominate American foreign policy in the twenty-first century.

The officers at the Chemical Division of USAREUR, who outnumbered the half-dozen enlisted men in the office, sought to persuade me to join the officer ranks. Having already turned down a similar invitation to attend officer candidate school after basic training, which would have entailed an extra year of duty, I was not even remotely tempted. My Harvard roommate Paul Russell had no similar choice. He was drafted as an officer after completing medical school and residency in 1961 and was posted as a physician to the 35th Field Artillery in a more rural town in Germany. In a letter he described military life from the point of view of a reluctant officer:

> Morale on the post is largely bad. The enlisted men particularly complain about everything, count the days until they leave this "hole." Even the officers form a tight little gossipy in-group and make little effort to extend themselves beyond the post. The enlisted men are interested in 1. women, 2. liquor. Needless to say, Americans are not well liked in Wertheim except for the money they bring in. Soldiers get drunk, destroy

> property, assault innocent people, rape German girls, and generally make themselves objectionable. General [Lucius} Clay [former American High Commissioner in Germany] established a midnight curfew for GI's in Germany which has done something to help matters.
>
> On top of this, there's a race problem. The town of Wertheim is considered "white"—not by the Germans who couldn't care less, but by the white enlisted men. Negroes are consigned to a much smaller farming village on the other side of the barracks. There have been a number of stabbings, most of which have arisen when a Negro, unaccompanied, goes into a "white" bar or restaurant. Sometimes they occur when a Negro strikes up a conversation with a German waitress, or is approached by a German prostitute, which the white EM thinks a violation of his supremacy.

Although few African Americans were stationed at USAREUR headquarters itself, there was considerable racial prejudice among the enlisted ranks in supporting units around Heidelberg. While there were no formal restriction at any of the German "GI joints" that catered to an American military clientele, African Americans risked humiliation or worse if they dared to enter a "white" bar.

Service in Germany had plenty of rewards, however. For one thing we no longer faced KP (kitchen police) duties, as low-wage German workers catered to our meal-time needs. We had to live on base (unless we had overnight or weekend passes), but the barracks of this former Wehrmacht *Kaserne*, now named after General George Patton, were far more comfortable than the spare wooden barracks at Ft. Leonard Wood. Some of us clandestinely rented rooms in town that could serve as a refuge during off-duty hours. Except for the area around the railroad station on the edge of town, which had been heavily bombed, Heidelberg had remained largely untouched by the war, apparently because the Allies had planned to use it for their headquarters after the German defeat (or, as others said, because of the popularity of the light opera *The Student Prince* in America). Hence plenty of rooms were available at ridiculously inexpensive prices for Americans, at an exchange rate of 4.5 marks to the dollar. I rented a succession of rooms, at first together with Tempy, who was enrolled at the University of Heidelberg, and later on my own. We decided to move out of our first room in the heart of the old city when our landlord stormed in one weekend at about noon while we were still in our beds. He pulled up the blinds, and indignantly exclaimed: "*Der Herrgott hat den Tag zur Arbeit geschaffen*" (God Almighty created the daytime for work). We attributed this outburst to his "typically German" moralism and narrow-mindedness. After several moves, one to the Uferstrasse on the other side of the Neckar, the river dividing the old city from later additions, I finally ended up in the spring of 1960 in a room fronting on the Hauptstrasse, the narrow and winding "main street" dating from medieval times. This I described at the time as "the finest room I've ever had, and exactly the kind of room I'd like to have forever...The windows facing out on the Hauptstrasse give me the enviable illusion of not missing anything, but still being apart, by myself." Today the Hauptstrasse is for pedestrian use only, but in those days the trolley still ran down the center of the street, producing a fierce clanging sound as it insistently pushed through traffic made heavier by the confined space in which drivers were forced to operate.

Drinking at Seppl's in Heidelberg with Tempy, Heidi, Leonore, and two student friends, 1959

The best thing about army service was the comradeship that inevitably develops among people facing shared trials, dangers, or hazards. This must be especially true in wartime when these shared ordeals involve life and death, which certainly wasn't the case for us in Heidelberg in 1959-1960, except when we, as competitive young males, deliberately and perversely risked our lives to demonstrate our courage. The imputations to which I have always been most allergic, perhaps because of the truth they contained, were those that accused me of "selfishness" and "spinelessness." One night I earned the admiration of my drinking buddies by recklessly crossing a cantilevered bridge on thirty-foot-high but only one-foot-wide steel arches on our way back to Patton Barracks. That feat required a sleepwalker's indifference to heights and a sure sense of balance. Even drinking "buddies" with whom I rarely got along had to acknowledge that I passed that particular *Mutprobe* (test of courage) with flying colors.

My closest friend was the Dartmouth graduate Jack Tansey, who had experienced American imperialism first-hand as the son of an American businessman in Venezuela. Jack taught us the slogan of the Cuban Revolution, "*Cuba si, Yanqui no*," which we enthusiastically adopted to express our disillusionment with military life.

With Jack Tansey and a student friend in Heidelberg, 1959

David Glazier, who played the guitar better than I did, defended the army in a back-handed way: "It's good that there is an institution for people such as this." David Burggraf was a high-strung, good-natured, well-spoken Midwestener, whose marriage was falling apart under the strains of military life. His passion when speaking for or against something he strongly felt and wanted desperately to get across gave me what I thought was an unflattering glimpse of myself. The youngest member of our group was the trombone-playing Jay Brackett, who had enlisted directly out of high school but felt instinctively drawn to our circle of older malcontents. Jay became something of a celebrity on the local Dixieland jazz scene, drawing a large group of young German fans to the *Cave* or the *Falle* (trap), where he was regularly invited to play. The hard-drinking, diminutive Pat Malloy was always at Jay's side, so loyal in his attendance that some of Jay's groupies assumed he must be a musician himself. Unable to convince a persistent fan that he did not play an instrument, Pat reported that the only way he could refuse the fan's entreaties was to tell him that he didn't *want* to play that night.

Joining us later in the year was David Coder, who would go on to earn a PhD in philosophy, and became the only one of my army buddies with whom I still remain in sporadic contact today. Jack Tansey described Dave as "always on the verge of despair," but he had the strength of his despair, deriving satisfaction from brooding about problems, both philosophical and practical. "He has none of that fidgety nervousness," I wrote in my journal, "or any of that antagonism that sensitive or introspective people often have." I particularly admired him for his seeming immunity to being made fun of. That some army types found him very strange did not faze him in the least. He considered it quite in order, displaying a strength of mind that I unsuccessfully tried to cultivate in myself. He did not feel being "different" was a failing, but accepted it with sturdy arrogance as a natural, even desirable fact. His father, an army chaplain in the rank of Lieutenant Colonel, was a dour, reticent, and strait-laced person. At David's invitation I visited his family in Neubrücke, where his father was stationed at the time. In my journal I described David`s father as a

> depressing sort of person, speaking hardly at all, but then only in the role of *Familienoberhaupt* (head of the family) and chaplain at the same time. A strong antipathy for his son's intellectualism is noticeable: "Son, why don't you come down to earth. You've got to learn to talk to the common man." A little bit of the army brutality has rubbed off on him too: "When are you going to get a haircut? Maybe I'd better whisper something in your CO's ear." And that in all seriousness! What Dave has from his father is that tendency to withdraw into himself, a thousand times more productive for him than for his father, no doubt. And also that pain-

> stakingly deliberate (and for his listeners nerve-wracking) way of talking. Every word is weighed, in true pulpit fashion, but unfortunately, at least in the father's case, the words don't seem to be any the better for the weighing...But David is strangely and wonderfully free of contempt for his family. He apparently never rebelled in so many words, but simply grew away from his family. His visits have almost a wistful tone—as if pleasant, relaxing reminders of a time long past...He never fights with his father, and when he laughs at him he is genuinely amused, not malicious...

David also visited us in Karlsruhe on his way back from a weekend motorcycle trip to Switzerland. His *schallendes Gelächter*, an enormously infectious laugh, was a great hit among the girls. His German was remarkably good for having studied it only for two years in school. And his deliberate delivery, sometimes so exasperating in English, was quite effective in German, where it could readily be laid to difficulties with a foreign language.

In September 1959 most of us at USAREUR went on a week-long military maneuver in a forested area near Orleans in France to test the effectiveness of our various assigned functions in a mock battlefield setting (this was several years before De Gaulle pulled France out of NATO to protest the Vietnam War). Here I was introduced to another rather uncommon army type.

> A CPX (command post exercise) that went wonderfully smoothly is over. The anticlimactic feeling on return is always part of it of course, but perhaps even more so this time, because it went so smoothly. Nightshift went fast with cookies, cigars, and midnight chow to help it along. Major Smith, a thoroughly lazy man, was easy to work with. He was so lazy he even felt it vicariously, and he tried to cut down the work for everybody. But he is honestly lazy; it's kind of a *Weltanschauung* with him, and there's no hypocrisy, no attempt to conceal it. There are lots of lazy people in the army, but too few of his kind—lazy on principle, openly, avowedly lazy. I say too few of his kind not because I really think that his kind has much to contribute, but rather because they serve as an effective corrective to the all-too-frequent pompous, aggressive, noise-making type of officer.

Throughout the year, three of my buddies—Jack, Jay, and Pat—and I saved up money and leave-time for a long-planned trip to Spain in the diminutive Fiat 500 I had bought in August 1959 from Colonel Bodé, my commanding officer at the Chemical Division at USAREUR.

Jay Brackett, Pat Malloy, and Jack Tansey at the start of our trip to Spain, April 1960

I had hoped my cousin Nick Edmonds, a talented artist recently posted to Friedberg in Germany, would be able to accompany us, but the Fiat turned out to be too small, and in any case, our schedules did not coincide. My three friends and I set off on our three-week journey in April 1960, only a month before Jack's and my long-awaited discharge from the army. Our tiny car was never quite up to the trip. We had our first mechanical troubles already in Alsace, shortly after crossing the French border.

Jack, Pat, and Jay powering my Fiat 500 to the nearest garage

Nonetheless, we made it to Spain, spending several days sight-seeing in Barcelona. Our original intention was to continue to Madrid, but the roads were so riddled with potholes that we could barely make it to Zaragoza, not even half-way to the capital. We spent the final week travelling down the Costa Brava to Tarragona and on to Valencia, with lots of minor adventures on the way. Jack spoke fluent Spanish, of course, having grown up in Latin America, but he was only rarely able to engage native Catalonians in political conversations in the urban areas of northeastern Spain. The signs of fascist rule were still everywhere. Uniformed paramilitary or police were posted at almost every street corner in Barcelona, keeping a wary eye on the citizenry in what had been the last Loyalist capital and the heart of anti-fascist resistance during the civil war.

Existentialist beatniks on the road

The four musketeers in Spain

My early release from the army, ostensibly to allow me to attend the University of Heidelberg, came on my 25th birthday, 8 May 1960. Jack and I, now free of all military obligations, spent the summer carousing in Heidelberg—mostly in the century-old student *Kneipen* (taverns) such as Seppl's and the *Rote Oxen* (which were not yet catering primarily to tourists)—before returning to the U.S. as civilians on a troopship in September of that year. That same month, in September 1960, my promotion to "specialist E-4" belatedly came through the Army pipeline, several months after my application had been submitted and three months after I had left the army. So much for the fabled efficiency of the military bureaucracy!

On 24 May 1960 Papa celebrated his fiftieth birthday (by the Gregorian calendar) in a grand black-tie ceremony that also served to mark his family's move into their splendid new home in the Durlach hills, overlooking the city of Karlsruhe several miles to the west. For almost a year the family had toured the construction site on weekends, watching the grand dimensions of his large and functional new home take shape. His comfortable wood- and leather-paneled office was set off from the living quarters by a long hall and plenty of space for secretaries and typists. The house itself had the obligatory wine cellar and a wet-bar that some years later would be moved into a more central location in the living room upstairs. Referring to the mirrors that fostered the illusion of an endless extension, Papa would call it the longest bar in the world. Shortly after this grand party I enthused in my journal about Papa:

> The most valuable lesson to learn from Papa is the grand manner, the opposite of pettiness. To forgive and forget is an example of this. To hold no grudges. To be generous, magnanimous. Never to make injurious remarks, never to insult. What was that definition of gentleman [from Galsworthy]? One who removes all obstacles to other persons' free and unembarrassed conduct. Live and let live. *Laissez faire.*

Papa hoped to persuade one of his children to study law, go into partnership with him, and eventually continue what he hoped would be a family dynasty at the *Bundesgerichtshof.*

Papa's daughters Sylvie, Stella, and Susanne, 1960

Who could have foreseen in those heady days that within another 50 years all of his children and grandchildren would have moved on from Karlsruhe and not a trace of his splendid new home in the *Rosengärtle* would remain? *Sic transit gloria.*

7
Boston, 1960-1962

The year-and-a-half that I spent in America between September 1960 and April 1962, when I again departed for Germany, this time for more than five years, marked in retrospect my last attempt to pursue a half-way normal career path. This was the plan, as recorded in my journal in Heidelberg in June 1960, shortly after my release from the army:

> My plans as they unfold: to return to America in September, work a year at BRS [Baldridge Reading Services], and go to grad school at Harvard in the fall. Each element of this plan has a preferable alternative, *zu dem ich mich nicht aber nicht entschliessen kann* (on which, however, I can't decide). Instead of returning in September, to remain over here, study in Paris, take another semester at Heidelberg or Munich. Instead of returning to BRS or grad school, to settle in New York or wherever and write. Both courses take a certain double or nothing daring...I wish I were somehow obviously incapable of making any sort of worldly success. Then I wouldn't be so tempted and distracted.

If I were allowed to choose only one point of my life to do over, to start anew, it would be after returning from Europe to the U.S. in the late summer of 1960 at the age of twenty-five. I should have stuck to my plans for graduate school, but for reasons that are still difficult to analyze and painful to recall I didn't do so. Instead, I gradually fell into a state of malaise and lethargy (similar, I thought, to John Bunyan's "slough of despond," although my "pilgrimage" was a very much more secular one) until I finally mustered the energy to at least try to recover a sense of purpose by once again transplanting my domicile to Germany.

My return to Baldridge Reading Services in September 1960 started auspiciously enough, despite some apprehensions recorded earlier in my journal:

> I will be better as a teacher when I get back to Reading Services. I won't be so shy and self-conscious about it as before. I'll know they're all playing a game and all they'll expect is that I play along. I'm a pretty good actor anyway, when I try. What will infuriate them is if I behave as if I question the validity or the value of the game.

Ken Baldridge and all of my colleagues were strong Kennedy supporters in this election year, which immediately struck a sympathetic chord with me, though I knew that my partiality was based only on partisan bias. "I'm for Jack Kennedy," I had written earlier that summer,

> Why? Because I feel an emotional attachment to the Democratic Party, and I'm inclined to love any Democrat. There is *no* rational basis for it. Certainly I could cite a number of policies, etc., in defense of my preference. For instance, off-shore oil, I think it should be given to "the people." All based on an attitude picked up somewhere along the way, probably from Mama. And I hate Republicans. That I think is more innate, more honest, more *a priori*, more rational in the sense that I can offer good critical reasons from a nucleus of conviction. I'd be more honest if I hated Democrats, too, but I can't. I'm too fond of them, I love them too much.

Later in the election season, on October 21st, I added the following comment, an instinctive reaction rather than one based on political analysis:

> Senator Kennedy certainly is a more capable man, more dynamic, more impressive than Nixon, but he plays to popular thought-clichés just as much, perhaps more skillfully: and the direction he's heading in is no different.

In the end I never got to vote for Kennedy, because I never settled in any location long enough to register to vote. My peripatetic life during the first few months after my return, traveling from one school to another, obviated the need to find a place of my own.

My first teaching assignment took me to Shady Side Academy in early October, at that time a posh prep school in Pittsburgh. Here in my spare time I mapped out a book rehearsing the many vaguely articulated discontents I had shared with my army buddies, but I left it at the planning stage and never followed through. Instead, I noted the inauthenticity of my present way of life and consoled myself for it:

> Review for a moment why you are here: For the money: The combination of light duties, plenty of leisure, expenses paid. Do not complain of being alone. The inevitability of that is one of the reasons you chose, or at least did not mind, returning to BRS. The extent to which you are unhappy is the extent to which you have been caught up, involved by your duties, the extent to which you have become, once again, a reading teacher and not Rodi.
>
> The paradox: I discourage taking the course too seriously (e.g., Sonia Lerner back at Pem-Day), and it hurts to see a student honestly worried about his or her reading. I encourage an attitude that "sees through" the reading program, but that continues conscientiously to go through the motions, as if there were a common understanding between teacher and student, "we both have our jobs, silly as they are, so let's do them." But when somebody draws the logical consequences from this attitude that I foster, then I'm lost, and all I can think of is, how can I hang on for a couple of weeks more and get out of here unscathed.

Under the influence of Camus' *The Rebel*, which I was reading at the time, I reached

> the unavoidable conclusion that I do not want absolute freedom; that I do not want choices to be completely arbitrary; but more than that, that I don't want choices to be completely personal preferences, but that I want these preferences to coincide with dictates outside and beyond me; that I avoid personal decisions. Then, of course, any choice or decision is a commitment and consequently a reduction in freedom. Only by a continuous suspension of decision can total freedom obtain. Total freedom then paradoxically precludes freedom of action by fostering continuous inaction. This is how total servitude, by obviating the necessity for personal decision, may give the illusion of total freedom.

> That slight feeling of shame at meeting other people, as if to say, "God, aren't we weak, spindly creatures in an absurd, chaotic condition." And then the feeling of having to ingratiate myself before he realizes that I have recognized him for what he is, the feeling of having to reassure him that I won't bring up the subject, that I'm much too interested in the "superficial aspect" of things.
>
> Camus begins at the stage that I have just barely reached: the "idea of the absurd." Awareness as I defined it in my letter to Betsy is little more than an appreciation of this idea. Camus: "Awareness...develops from every act of rebellion: the sudden, dazzling perception that there is something in man with which he can identify himself, even if only for a moment."

Camus even influenced my take on the election:

> Long argument over breakfast on Kennedy-Nixon, specifically the meaning and significance of anti-Catholicism. I suggested that it might be more accurate to view the conflict as not between Protestant and Catholic, but between non-religious and religious. The danger that people see in Kennedy's Catholicism is that he will make his decisions according to absolute and rigid religious principles, as enunciated by a church with a tradition of success in enforcing application of rigid principles in day-to-day affairs. The argument that Nixon is a Quaker, hence a member of a sect that preaches non-violence, is easily countered: his supporters say, in effect, that he isn't really a good Quaker and that he won't allow religious principles to interfere with day-to-day decisions. Protestantism is safely shallow in America today; religion made innocuous. Although I sympathize with the religious attitude, although I lean to it and often have to fight my way back to common sense and lucidity, I nevertheless appreciate the dangers of the religious attitude in politics. It is, to paraphrase Camus, thought that recognizes no limits. Opposition to a Catholic as president in this sense, intolerance for the sake of tolerance, is healthy. What is sickening is the hypocrisy with which [Kennedy's critics] conceal their lack of religion.

Immediately after the end of the Shady Side program in early November I was dispatched on a lengthy sales trip through the Midwest. My schedule was designed to allow me to celebrate Thanksgiving with Olaf and Cora in Minneapolis, a festive occasion at which our cousin, John Edmonds, then an undergraduate at near-by Carleton College, also participated. The weather was warm enough for a touch football game, during which I lost my signet ring (a hand-me-down from Papa's second wife, Halinka), miraculously retrieved by collective effort after what initially seemed like a hopeless search. Memories of this holiday were marred, however, when a few days later, in early December, Olaf's second son Peter, born 1959, had to be rushed to the emergency room at the University of Minnesota Medical School with acute meningitis. Fortunately, an experimental treatment involving removal of the affected membrane of the brain proved to be successful. My young nephew survived the usually fatal disease. Whether there were lasting after-effects that may have contributed to Peter's tragically early death in 1997 remains an unanswered question.

My visits to Olaf, fixed as he was on an academic career that would eventually take him to a dozen productive years on the faculty at Duke University and then to the chairmanship of the mathematics department at Kent State for over twenty years, always revived my yearning for academic life. After a previous visit to Minneapolis while on leave from the army after basic training in 1958 I had written:

> In looking back [in my journal] I saw an entry, during my Columbia period, of stultifying class atmosphere. How differently I felt when touring the Minnesota campus with Olaf! A whole five or ten city blocks devoted just to intellectual endeavor! A feeling that of course only over-extended absence could engender.

Nonetheless, for reasons that are still painful to recall, I botched my chance to return to academic life as a graduate student in the German department at Harvard in the fall of 1961. I was indeed reaccepted at Harvard, though without an offer of a teaching assistantship, which meant I had to finance graduate studies on my own, at least for the first year. Not coincidentally, I abruptly quit on the day, a couple of weeks into the semester, on which my first tuition payment fell due. But it would be wrong to leave the impression that finances forced me to abandon graduate school. A nice financial offer from BRS to continue working for them certainly influenced my decision (after a childhood in poverty I have always felt an almost pathological need to save money rather than to spend it, earning me the probably deserved reputation as a miser), but it was my own lack of commitment to teaching (or at least teaching German language and literature) as a profession that was at the source of my (in)decision. I had lingering ambitions of becoming a free-lance writer. I foolishly divulged this reservation about joining the academic profession to the head of the department, Stuart Atkins, who warned me that this was "no field for dilettantes." In my journal I deplored "the flatness of my colleagues in the German Department (by looks and sounds anyway)" and "the pointlessness of it all looming up (especially in Middle High German , where it's combined with difficulty)." I came to the realization that "I want Harvard only to gain a position of 'strength'—from there I can throw more dynamite." A few days later I bemoaned

> my inability to meet my fellow students—who of course have all met each other already. There's no common ground to meet on: the German Dept. isn't common ground; skepticism about it would be!
>
> I have an anti-Harvard rebellious and skeptical instinct. Can I last through the year with it? If I can, the insights that derive therefrom may serve me in very good stead. I view Germanistik too much as a profession: they realize it and hold that against me. My insight infects me. Those that don't have that insight simulate ingenuous, sincere interest in the subject, and no ulterior motive for study.

As much as my abrupt departure from Harvard in October 1961 may seem like an ill-advised snap decision from my perspective as a retired college teacher half a century later, it was well prepared long beforehand by a festering ambivalence about academic life, as attested by this journal entry while still teaching "speed reading" at Shady Side Academy in October 1960:

> The practice of literary criticism assumes acceptance and participation in the life of the world. It dissects literature for values useful to the world, and applies existing values to literature. The practice of "creative writing" assumes at least a partial rejection of the life of the world, a self-sufficiency, a closed universe. This explains why such a vast number of highly talented people spend their lives on literary criticism (and teaching) instead of on "creative writing." It is <u>not</u> a matter of insufficient talent, but rather a case of conscious preference. The struggle for recognition, for intellectual power, far from being diminished, is magnified. Literary

critics get more fame and remuneration than literary artists, within their lifetimes, that is.

Do I choose literary criticism by returning to Harvard? No. I'm throwing anchor and seeking a means of support, and access to the great library. I have no illusions about feeling any more comfortable in an academic vocation than in any other.

Meanwhile I had already thrown a bit of an anchor in Boston, living with my slightly younger Edmonds cousins Nick, Liz, and later Ellen at 25 Elmer Street in Cambridge, long since displaced by one of Harvard's newer undergraduate Houses. Later we moved to Blackwood Street off Massachusetts Avenue in Boston. Both were at that time urban neighborhoods in decline. We were all determined to live as cheaply as possible, not moving from our very low-rent Elmer Street apartment until a cockroach infestation literally drove us out. I was the last hold-out, rather enjoying the urban slum. Nick, who went on to a career as a prize-winning sculptor in the Fine Arts department at Boston University, was a hard-working student at the Museum School in Boston, and Liz, who later trained as a teacher of the deaf, was completing her undergraduate degree at BU. My move to the Boston area was facilitated by Ken Baldridge's willingness to allow me to work part time in the BRS Boston office, headed by a distant descendant of a famous Boston family, Peter Bent Brigham III, partially disabled in a youthful hunting accident. To reduce his rental costs he and his wife Natalie at one time contemplated moving to our Elmer Street apartment house—until I told them about the cockroaches (but not about the fleas)!

At Elmer Street I used my spare time to do some desultory writing, translating Bertolt Brecht just for fun. His mordant, anti-militarist protest poetry perfectly fitted my unsettled frame of mind that summer. It was quite a challenge to keep the bite without losing the mellifluous rhythm and rhyme of the original. Having always, along with my siblings, taken great pleasure in scatological humor, I particularly liked his poem, "Orge's Song."

Orge said to me:
The place that's dearest to him here on earth
Is not his parents' grave or place of birth.
The place he laid the greatest weight upon

on earth was always, as he said, the john.
For here's a place one calmly can endure
that overhead are stars and underneath manure.
A place is simply wonderful, where one,
if one is adult, can be quite alone.
A place of humbleness, where you learn with a sting
that you are just a man, who may not keep a thing.
A place where, though the body is at rest,
one gently, but with pressure, does what's best.
A place of wisdom where you can prepare
your belly so there's room for more in there.
You realize what you are without conceits:
A fellow, sitting on the john, who – eats.

I also tried my hand at some poetry of my own. "The Buddy Shot" was based on an incident during my basic training:

"In case of gas attack you gotta act fast:
This little syringe here can save your buddy's life,
If given fast, right through his clothes and all.
Today you'll learn just how to give these shots.
First you will shoot your buddy; in the thigh.
Then he'll shoot you; there's nothing to the thing.
It doesn't hurt, that's if you do it right;
It <u>will</u> hurt if you don't."
Thus spoke the seargeant, brandishing the needle –
Lethal (if looks could kill).
All went about the job with great efficiency,
Stabbing and being stabbed. Only one seemed
Incapable of administering the shot.
Hands trembling, taut and white:
Twice, three, four times; his jabs were much too faint.
The sergeant, supervising, was provoked:
The stabbing hurt the stabbed and not the stabber!
Unable now to handle this emergency,
He hailed the Master Sergeant.
Authority ingrained, his order chiseled, blunt:

"Now hold that needle right here, four inches up.
When I say 'jab', jab hard and all the way.
Now jab." This time it worked,
And all around were visibly relieved.
His buddy smiled and said, "it didn't hurt."
But all those tentative jabs had drawn some blood.
The sergeant, like a beast, wild at the sight of blood,
Commands the buddy now, whose turn it is,
To jab as he'd been jabbed.
"Feel it?" the sergeant asks, triumphant in his rage.
But the recruit is all in smiles by now,
As calm in suffering pain as he had been
Taut, nervous in inflicting.
They could have jabbed all day, he wouldn't have cared.

That summer I also made good friends with Charlotte Willard, a Jewish refugee from Austria before the war now in her early 40s and working in an office next to BRS. She had never quite recovered from her traumatic expulsion from her native land and spoke with surprising nostalgia and great feeling of her interrupted youth in Vienna. Unlikely as it might seem in view of our different backgrounds, we shared a sense of being uprooted and a generalized disillusionment with our present lives, manifested in Charlotte's case by a caustic wit and refreshing irreverence. Charlotte told me she could tell right away whether a person was neurotic or not: "I can tell by their appearance." I asked her whether she could tell from my appearance whether I was neurotic. "Oh, I'd have to go back to when I first met you," she answered. "I know you too well now. Now I *know* you are." She cautioned me not to think of writing in my present state of nerves, or I'd be taken to the hospital on a stretcher as she had been at one time, paralyzed on one side. "*Viel Größere als du sind schon verhungert*" (many greater ones than you have died of hunger), she warned. The source of her own ill health turned out to be a brain aneurysm not definitively diagnosed until the late 1960s.

One of Charlotte's friends was the regular house-sitter for Henry Kissinger, then a young professor at Harvard, and she occasionally invited us over to his modest, but comfortable 1950s-style split-level suburban home when he was away. I recall seeing the manuscript of his book on nuclear war (later that year to be published as *Necessity for Choice*) on his desk, a jolting reminder of how different (and, as I thought, greater) my ambition was than his, and how dilatory I had become in pursuing my goal of writing "the great American novel". A few years later, in Berlin, I experienced a related false epiphany when I first read the news that Robert F. Kennedy was considering running for the presidency against LBJ in the mid-sixties. What remarkable self-restraint, I thought. Wasn't it much more fulfilling and also more important to write a good book? How dedicated to public service one must be to so easily renounce private satisfactions!

The major event in my personal life in the summer of 1961 was a terrible row I had with Mama in Vermont. My relations with her had soured while I was still far away in the army in Germany. I held it against her that she had written a letter to Tempy in Heidelberg—unaware, perhaps, that we were sharing a room at the time—in which she never mentioned my name, but made what seemed like a gratuitous reference to me: "The common man counts for much more than the occasional Harvard man," or something innocuous to that effect. Sweety Degenfeld, with whom Tempy had spent much time in Hinterhör after his arrival in Germany in 1958, had just visited her daughter in America, meeting with Mama and Ginny Biddle in New York on the way, and evidently the letter reflected not only Sweety's very appreciative report of how charmed she was by Tempy, but also her (and Mama's) concern about Tempy's uncertain future, especially if he continued on his current erratic path in Germany. In retrospect, the letter was an effort to encourage Tempy (who did not return to the U.S. until 1963) to pursue his education more seriously and not to be discouraged by the apparent magnitude of the task. Excluded as I was from all greetings and salutations, I took the letter as a deliberate slight.

I drew an entirely unwarranted lesson from this minor incident: in the competition for parental attention and affection, it pays to be "bad" rather than "good" (a form of sibling rivalry well-described in John Steinbeck's *East of Eden*, and, more subtly, in Eugene O'Neill's *Long Day's Journey into Night*). Only later I learned that parents, especially mothers, are almost congenitally unable to withhold love from any of their offspring, but are also strongly programmed to give help to those of their children who needed it most. This was the psychological background to the terrible fight I had with my mother in the summer of 1961. I have, no doubt, always had something of a "mother complex." Years later I recall the genuine shock of my father-in-law Gerhard Heuss, who in his serious German way had developed a superficial expertise in various branches of pop psychology. On a visit to Steffi and me in far-away San Diego in 1976 he looked at some doodles he had instructed me to make on a piece of paper. Never in all of his long experience had he seen such a clear case of maternal fixation! In his eyes I was in serious trouble if I did not succeed in weaning myself from my subconscious wish to return to the womb. So I suppose my row with Mama fifteen years earlier may be seen as a cathartic (but never entirely successful) effort to liberate myself from her domination! And indeed her approval remained for the rest of my life my highest criterion for a thing well done.

On returning from Germany in September 1960, I had made little effort to contact Mama. A visit to her seemed out of the question as I was constantly on the road for BRS and, on moving to Boston, had sold my own car (the Fiat 500) for a pittance in an effort to downsize my expenses. Mama had settled on her remote and primitive farmstead in northern Vermont. Living with her was a younger distant relative, Johnny White, the victim of a frontal lobotomy—still a common treatment for chronic depression at the time. She had made an arrangement with his family to take him in for a small fee for room and board. Later they were joined by Connie Sherwin, whom Mama met through her niece Ginny Biddle in New York. An imposing figure at well over six feet in height and butch to the core, Connie had inherited a bit of wealth which she was willing to invest in Mama's always somewhat chimerical agrarian projects. Their relationship was anything but harmonious, however, mainly due to Connie's chronic alcoholism, which would eventually lead to her early death in 1970.

Meanwhile, our social life at Elmer Street involved trips to the sprawling Edmonds family "estate" on Reservation Road in nearby Andover nearly every weekend. Here we not only enjoyed Aunt Temple's marvelous home cooking, but also, at 5 o'clock every afternoon, the highly convivial cocktail hours presided over by Uncle John in the smoke-filled library. It was in the company of Aunt Temple and Uncle John in early June 1961 that I visited Mama for the first time since returning from Germany in September 1960. It was not a successful visit. Mama directed Johnny White's heavily sarcastic wit, sitting back and watching it hit home: for instance when he called Aunt Temple (who, as always, came laden with gifts) "Santa Claus," or in innumerable snide comments to me, such as, "you really get around." This conspiratorial understanding between Mama and Johnny got under Aunt Temple's skin as well. In relations between the two sisters power was always at stake, and gifts never came without unspoken strings attached. I remember Aunt Temple once anticipating a rare visit by Mama to Reservation Road (on her way to Vermont): "I hope she doesn't bring me a goat." She made no apologies for her own genuine need to help rescue or rehabilitate people, whether Hungarian immigrants or impoverished relatives: "To me that is life, that is living." On 16 June 1961 I recorded my impression of our trip to the north in my journal:

> Post-mortem on the visit to Mama in Vermont: although I had planned to stay a few extra days, I left with Aunt Temple, after customary vacillation. What made it terrible was that I had earlier told Mama that I didn't have to be at work until Monday. It was not as if I had planned from the start not to stay. Nor could I invent a very satisfactory excuse: only that I wanted to save money. Under the circumstances it was about the most cruel thing I could do to her. Looking back in the car, I saw Mama and Johnny standing, not waving, just looking, the picture of being left behind. Why didn't I stay?
>
> Because being in Mama's home for any length of time gives me the same feeling as I used to get at the end in the *Falle* [in Heidelberg]: dead end. No future, only past, and gradual, but irrevocable deterioration. I don't think Mama has changed much, it's probably me, but she struck me as somehow more defeated, and perhaps because I feel the same thing in myself so strongly, I long for the light and escape, like a drowning man gasping for breath. Aunt Temple and Papa are the opposite [of Mama]—paragons of good health—and it would have been very difficult for me to stand with Johnny and Mama and wave the Andover station wagon goodbye.
>
> There's more to it than that, but that gets at the essence. In the back of my mind were the tennis games I had planned for this weekend [with Charlotte], the cocktails in Andover, and petty little things like that, fear of being put to work, disgust at lack of toilet facilities, etc. But the real reason was that I didn't want to be absorbed into that nature-loving, impersonal resignation, that wistful, only <u>half</u>-healthy-minded, only <u>half</u>-

rebellious intelligence, that physical working and working and working at nothing.

I was quite wrong about Mama's health. Living alone for her last 28 years until she died in her own bed in 1998 at age 86, she would outlive her two years-older former husband by five years and her four years-older sister by a full fifteen. Accustomed as I was to thinking of health as unavoidably precarious, and worried about Mama's lack of insurance (at least until Social Security and Medicare kicked in when she turned 62 in 1974), I asked what she would do if she got sick. Impatiently she answered, "get well again."

My relations with Mama never improved much from that point on. Later that summer, visiting her and Connie on my own (Johnny White was not present), we had the bad fight referred to earlier. The three of us had been drinking heavily and recriminations were freely exchanged. At one point Mama told me never to come again. Connie, in her thankless role as a third party to an obviously long-festering family conflict, took me aside and told me Mama hadn't really meant what she said. I was always welcome to visit and she hoped I would come again soon.

In September of that year, I heard more specifically from Betsy what Mama held against me, although I really knew it all the time. By then Betsy had been banished by Aunt Temple from Reservation Road for forming an excessively close relationship with her cousin Nick (Aunt Temple's son) and distracting him from his work. Betsy had perforce established herself with her twins (then in their terrible twos), on the opposite side of the state of Vermont from Mama, in Burlington, where she planned to continue her music studies while working at some boring day-time job. "What Mama doesn't like about you," Betsy told me, "is that you won't sacrifice yourself to your writing, that you won't make any sacrifices, like living in Vermont, being hard on yourself for a year or two. You still have a chance—she still hates you. She's going after Tempy, hook, line, and sinker."—"Sort of a different situation than you expected between Mama and me, isn't it?" I asked. "Yes," Betsy said. "Before you came up to Vermont I always thought you were the stronger one. Now I realize that she is."

When my Edmonds cousins and I moved to Blackwood Street later that autumn (after I had aborted my return to Harvard), I began to frequent a bar called "Casey's" on Mass Ave on the opposite side of Symphony Hall. Here I met an alcoholic woman of Irish descent named Terry Fortes, who had long since been abandoned with her three children by their aberrant African-American father. "Sit down," Terry encouraged me. "The work'll be there after you're gone," or, "Live it up, you'll be dead a long time." One of her favorite expressions was, "What time does the balloon go up?" I took the oldest of her children, twelve year-old Jimmy, under my wing. This led to some conflict at Blackwood Street, as Jimmy and his friends were always around, and my cousins found my close relationship with Jimmy exploitative and unhealthy. It finally dawned on me that they were probably right. My attraction to Jimmy was probably not as altruistic and disinterested as it might have seemed to me at the time. Charlotte suspected me of being a little bit *andersherum* ("other way around"), as she politely put it—the term "gay" then still being reserved exclusively for use in its original sense. The need to end a relationship that could easily be misconstrued helped convince me to return to Europe the following spring.

In January 1962 I went up to Vermont to celebrate Mama's 50th birthday. What a contrast to Papa's posh black-tie 50th party in Karlruhe two years before! In Vermont it was a raucous affair, involving not only Connie and Johnny White, but also numerous colorful Vermont characters from the surrounding countryside whose company Mama particularly enjoyed. She recognized her weakness for eccentric individuality, admitting she had never been "discriminating" in her choice of friends. She seemed to be hoping and apprehensively expecting that Ginny, at that time a physician in training at Columbia Medical School, might put in a surprise appearance to cap the evening. One of Mama's seedy guests, too drunk, or perhaps too lazy (or too cold in the freezing weather), to visit the outhouse in the hall connecting the back of the house to the barn, defecated on the front porch without even a hint of embarrassment. Most of her guests left peacefully, as guests usually do, but some had to be firmly escorted out, others carried and packed into their cars, or into any car heading in their direction.

A few months later, when I was already back in Germany, Mama referred to this party in a letter to encourage me in my writing:

> I think you could make some money, a potboiler, with your idea of comparing Papa's birthday and mine. That's the kind of semi-sentimental, semi-comic stuff that magazines like. Go ever so superficially into the profounder motivations of each birthday person and call it "Search for a Yankee," or just the opposite, or some such nonsense—

She also urged me to learn the Zither to augment my untutored guitar skills (I had briefly taken some classical guitar lessons while in the army, but gave them up so as not to miss out on partying with my buddies). She urged me to look up Paul Kiem (1882-1960), alias Kiem Pauli, whose collections of Bavarian folk songs she had grown to love during her years in Germany. However, to my great retrospective regret, I never followed up on her well-intended advice.

Before I could leave for Germany I had one more assignment to fulfill for Baldridge Reading Services, a six-week developmental reading course at—of all places—Ursuline Academy for Girls in New Orleans. In the summer of 1961 I had enjoyed six weeks of relief from the urban grime conducting a program at Exeter Academy in New Hampshire. New Orleans was to be my final station with BRS. I had actually sold the program to the Ursulines on one of my sales trips, so I was a logical candidate to conduct the program there as well. I rented an apartment (in old slave quarters) at 821 Toulouse Street in the French Quarter and used every opportunity to explore the city and the night life. During the day I traveled by bus to the school in the northern part of the city, where I was treated with great respect but kept segregated from the girls during meal times. On the day after Colonel John Glenn became the first American to orbit the earth (20 February 1962), Mother Elizabeth asked me incredulously, "After something wonderful like yesterday, how can there still be people who don't believe in God?"

From a Redemptorist nun at a school in the south of the city, to whom I tried to sell the reading program, I learned something about the socio-economic ruptures in the Catholic community. She wouldn't even be able to refer her students to Sacred Heart or Ursuline, because her pupils were stigmatized:

> "I'm sure the madams of the Sacred Heart wouldn't welcome one of our kids. The people who go to those schools wouldn't talk to anyone from this district."—"But I thought this was the Garden District?"—"Oh, my, no. That's a couple of blocks up. From Magazine to St. Charles is the Garden District. From Magazine down to the river is our channel district. Magazine St. is the dividing line. People from the other side wouldn't even cross the street to go to church here. That's the real old-time Southern upper crust. Not the wealthy ones, they live out by the lake. In fact, some of these people in the Garden District are dirt poor. Yet they wouldn't

> send their children to us. They send'em to Ursuline or Sacred Heart. And they got no right to. I know a woman who's living hand to mouth, just barely getting by. Yet she's planning to send her daughter to Ursuline next year. Now she's got no right to. She can't afford that. She should send that child here, where the tuition costs $90 for the whole year, not just the uniform like it does at Ursuline. But she'll send her to Ursuline just for the prestige. That's the way it is down here. New Orleans is the biggest small town in the world."—"That's interesting that there should be such strict lines drawn. What about the French Quarter, is that supposed to be fashionable?"—"Polluted. It's fashionable for entertainment at certain hours. The highbrows dine at St. Antoine's, but they don't want to be seen in the Quarter after 10 o'clock. Then the lowbrows take over. And only the people who work the Quarter live there, and other motley characters."

Mardi Gras came late that year, in early March. I spent the day on a vodka-induced high, dancing in the streets from one tavern to another. Behind me a troop of tourists formed, taking me for a native who would lead them to all the hot spots in the Quarter. And, indeed, I took considerable satisfaction that I was already initiated enough into the New Orleans scene to gain automatic admission to hip joints like the Gaslight Tavern off Bourbon Street, where visitors attracted by the great nightly jazz had to stand for hours and pay to get in. My reception by other habitués wasn't always that warm, of course. One night, irritated by the same old question, "Where do you come from?" I answered, "What difference does it make? I dropped from heaven." My inquisitor took offense: "Another of those guys. Really think you're something, don't you? Beatnik dropped from heaven into the heart of New Orleans jazz. You make me sick."

My landlady, however, appreciated me. She had a fit one night because the man in the apartment next door threw a party, and some of the guests got drunk and made noise.

> "Somebody ought to shoot you," she said to one of them at one point. This morning she apologized to me for the noise. I told her it didn't bother me. "Oh, you're so kind, Mr. Stackelberg," she said. "I'm tellin' you I was so nervous I was cryin'. He told me he was only havin' a couple people over, but then they brought two more, and they brought two more, and you know how it is. There was dancin' and everything. I'm gonna speak

> to him. I don't care if he moves out, he's not gonna do that again. You rent a hall some place if you want a party like that. Oh, life sure is tough, ain't it?"—"Well, I don't think that's the toughest part."—"Oh, you're so kind, Mr. Stackelberg."

My last days in Boston were haunted by odd dreams. I dreamt at one point of a map in which Europe and America connected at a single point in Albany, Vermont. In another one Mama had sent me her old tattered passport. The implication was that she wanted to come to Europe with me. In mid-April I made a last goodbye-visit to Vermont, and this time I stuck it out, letting Mama do all the talking. It seemed to me she was trying to direct my gaze outside of myself, knowing I would never write anything of any quality unless I could learn to do so. Johnny White was on his way out of the Vermont threesome, having finally managed to get on everyone's nerves as a result of his compromised mental and social functions.

In transit to my steamer to Europe on April 19th I called Jack Tansey in New York to bid him goodbye. He complained bitterly about the dreariness of his present life as an executive trainee and said he wished he could join me. I commiserated with him, but I never saw or spoke to him again. In my journal I regretted that once again "the scissor is applied to my life."

8
BERLIN, 1962-1964

In late April 1962 Tempy welcomed me back to Heidelberg sporting a beard—one that soon came off when he realized I had not followed through on my own resolution to grow a beard after New Orleans. Through his good offices I rented an excellent room in the courtyard of a grand turn-of-the-century mansion on the Klingenteichstrasse, half-way up the road to the famous castle ruins that attract so many visitors to the town. Tempy had enrolled at Heidelberg University, but less for the sake of study than to join the *Saxo-Borussia*, an aristocratic Prussian student "corps" loosely affiliated with the traditional German Baltic fraternity, *Dorpatensis* (named after the Estonian university town Dorpat, today Tartu). The *Saxo-Borussia* boasted a long line of high-born former student members, including, before the war, two of Kaiser Wilhelm II's sons.

In August 1960, at the tender age of 21, Tempy had married the charming and attractive Brigitte Eisenhardt, henceforth known in the family as "Bridge." Mama would later proclaim her "the family beauty," a judgment with which no one could disagree. Tempy had met her in Paris the previous year, and they immediately hit it off. Tempy's letters, always high-spirited, reached a peak of enthusiasm previously unmatched. Tempy was obviously head-over-heels in love. A few months later they were engaged, and the wedding took place at Bridge's parents' home in Bad Nauheim. I thought he was a bit young for such a venture, and perhaps vulnerable to an older woman's social ambitions, but I was very aware that my reservations could easily be put down to the jealousy, or even envy, of a three-years-older brother who had no such wildly romantic prospects. In any case I knew that any effort to dissuade him from marrying would have the opposite effect. I felt I was driving him toward her as it was—not by anything I said, but from the growing distance between us. From my half-sisters I reaped no gratitude for suggesting to Papa that he give the young couple a second-hand car for their wedding—a present they would surely need as they prepared for at least temporary employment at cousin Karl Georg's Emnid Institute in Bielefeld (closely affiliated with the American Gallup public opinion poll).

When I returned to Heidelberg in April 1962, I found Tempy heavily involved in the corps. This was a *schlagende Verbindung*, a fraternity that still practiced the traditional rites of sword dueling as in the nineteenth century. Although some of the dueling fraternities welcomed facial scars, traditional symbols of courage in the face of danger, the Saxo-Borussia had moved beyond that primitive stage. Striking below the eyes was no longer permitted, so the scars from these ritualized duels often remained invisible above the hairline. In any case, the purpose of dueling was not necessarily to "win," as in sports, but to practice discipline and solidarity. Much more important than gaining the upper hand in combat or inflicting a wound on one's opponent was not to flinch or duck when one's opponent struck. Rising to the challenge—some demonstration of Hemingway's "grace under pressure"—is what really counted. As in so many aspects of German culture, cowardice was the vice to be exorcized. The dialectically conditioned effect of this and other rituals, however, was to promote conformity to inherited group norms, and thus, in the last analysis, to weaken civic courage and political dissent.

Ritualized drinking served much the same purpose as dueling. The object was not necessarily to drink as much as one could but to learn how to hold one's liquor. Organized drinking bouts in full corps regalia—the so-called *Kneipen* or more formal *Kommers*—not only fostered conviviality, but served to train and test members' ability to conduct themselves graciously in social situations. Great value was placed on humor as the disposition most likely to lead to equanimity, chivalry, and friendship. But humor of a more withering kind was meted out to those who didn't measure up to the demanding ethos of the corps.

From the start Tempy had difficulty coordinating the demands of the corps with the duties of marriage. The corps consumed most of his time and left Bridge feeling neglected. Bridge's attitude toward the corps was ambivalent. There is no doubt she got satisfaction from Tempy's aristocratic status and the attentions of his aristocratic friends. She told me that she would have liked to have been a *Hofdame*, holding court, "*den Ton angeben und die Sprache pflegen*" (setting the tone and cultivating the language). According to Tempy, Bridge really loved the corps, even if she wouldn't admit it, but Sweety Degenfeld told me that she hated it. I thought Bridge rather resented my access through Tempy to corps "secrets." Either I could be outside and criticize, or I could be inside and appreciate, but to be both inside and outside, as it were—no, that was not permissible. My own attitude toward the corps was quite defensive:

> They produce, by their way of life, by their activities certain pleasurable feelings—comradeship, belonging, elite membership, honorable, admirable, traditional life, courage in dueling, continuity (false eternity), avoidance of boredom, etc., etc. By my way of life, so completely different, I do the same thing—produce certain pleasurable feelings, but of a different kind: the corps kind don't satisfy enough. My way of life has a safety-valve built in: no matter what misfortune befalls me, I can always analyze it.

One of the first events I attended on returning to Germany was Sweety's festive 80th birthday celebration at Hinterhör on 25 May 1962. It was a ceremonious occasion, befitting the great esteem in which she was held by her wide circle of friends from every sphere of life, not least the theatre and the arts. In 1974, four years after her death at age 87, her extensive correspondence with the Austrian poet and playwright Hugo von Hofmannsthal (1874-1929) was published (and translated into English in 2000). Begun after the death of her husband in 1908 and carried on for more than twenty years, their correspondence revealed a rich interior life and a degree of intimacy between them that few had previously suspected.

On 28 May 1962 I recorded an embarrassing incident in Hinterhör in my journal:

> Saturday afternoon Sweety found Tempy and me alone in the *Halle* and immediately used the opportunity: "You know that I saw Mama in America. I was ill, I thought I would die, I lay in bed and could hardly speak. Poor Mama had to drive eight hours, and then we could only talk for two hours.

> *"Also, Kinder, sie hat mir so leid getan, in der Seele leid getan"* (children, I felt so sorry for her, sorry in my soul). *Kinder, ihr müsst was werden, und sei es nur ein Schmied, ihr müsst etwas werden* (children, you have to become something, if only a blacksmith, you have to make something of yourselves). If you want to save her spiritual existence, you have to make something of yourselves. After all, she is reproached from all sides for doing something wrong with you, for somehow failing you. She just wants to be able to say, 'see, the children did turn out well.' She would never admit that is what she wants, but one can feel it, one can sense it. She spoke about Olaf all the time, how well he's doing, how he is now getting his doctorate. Again and again she returned to this subject. I thought to myself, what is the matter with her, just a minute ago she twice told me the same thing. Children, she can only justify herself through you. Only you can prove that her upbringing was right after all."
>
> My first reaction was rage and I spit out something mean, *"sie ist doch selber nichts geworden"* (she never made anything of herself, either). Sweety ignored it and said something about *"ihr seid doch Männer"* (but you are men), when fortunately we were interrupted.
>
> Later she saw me standing disconsolately. She called me over to her, asked me first what I was doing now, then said her strictures had been meant mainly for Tempy. *"Er ist doch ihr Pet, das weisst du doch* (he is her pet, you know that). I believe Tempy thinks Mama likes the Bohemian life. But that is not so. She would say that she likes it, but she doesn't inside. And one has to make that clear to Tempy."

But clearly the message was intended for me as well.

Mama's misfortunes did not end with the stress inflicted on her by her wayward sons (or by her even more contrary daughter). That winter—in January 1963—her farm in Vermont burned to the ground, with the loss of about twenty cows, calves, and other livestock. Electric wiring exposed to the elements or dangling along the ground and the absence of any safety precautions made an accident almost inevitable. The fire started in the barn and spread throughout the house before the first fire fighters arrived. Among its other effects, the fire drastically changed the power relations on the farm. Connie Sherwin now assumed the proprietorship. She bought the neighboring farm with all its livestock. Knowing nothing about farming—she didn't even know how to milk a cow—she hired Mama to operate the farm. In theory this was to be an equal partnership, Connie furnishing the capital and Mama the know-how and labor, but in practice it was Connie who now called all the shots.

Meanwhile, back in Heidelberg, I was drawn to my own group of friends, quite different from Tempy's. They were mostly theology students, a bit younger than me. I met them at the *Weinloch*, a marvelously shabby student drinking spot that has always looked like it was on its last legs, but is still going strong half a century later. I struck up friendships with the students and we spent many long hours talking about the meaning of life and other weighty matters, just like back in college. Here I also renewed my acquaintance with the long-haired *Munke*, the pseudonym of local artist and muralist Rainer Motz (1934-1990), whom I had gotten to know back in my army days. After a drunken night in the *Falle* in the summer of 1959, I had woken up in his bed in his charming little studio in Rohrbach, a rural suburb of Heidelberg, in the morning. I resisted his advances after that, with greater or lesser success, but we remained good friends. Interestingly, all the homosexual encounters in my life seemed only to confirm that this was *not* what I wanted.

Munke at a party in his backyard studio in Rohrbach, 1960

The *Weinloch* was also where I met Ingrid, a country girl from a small village between Heidelberg and Karlsruhe. Her real name was Ingeborg

Kaiser, but she always used "Ingrid" with me to signal what she hoped would be a total break from her previous life. She was only 20, six years younger than me, but she had been and still was married when I met her and had a one-year-old son. Her health was fragile, but her lust for life was great. While on a prescribed *Kur* at a health resort, a few months before I got to know her, she had foolishly started a romance with a fellow patient. Ingrid's husband discovered their intense correspondence and sued for divorce. Under the punitive German system in force at the time, Ingrid lost the suit and all rights to her child. I tried to help and comfort her. This was the most sensuous relationship I had had up to that time in my life, and I was very much in love. I was attracted not only by her sensuality, but also her simplicity, and her weakness for fantasy. We were both catching up on something we had missed out on in our teenage years. But the relationship was doomed, although it took more than a year to disintegrate. In early December Ingrid's ex-husband used his power over the child to force Ingrid to sleep with him. It was a dereliction I could never forgive. Ironically, Ingrid had not really missed her son—until she had fallen in love again.

In Heidelberg, 1962

We tried to save the relationship by moving to Berlin. We arrived in the war-torn and divided city in January 1963 late in the evening in one of the coldest winters on record. There were absolutely no rooms to be had. We finally lied our way into an overcrowded youth hostel, even though at age 27 I was no longer eligible to make use of its residential facilities. There were shortages of everything in Berlin, not just rooms, but also jobs. The wall had gone up only a year-and a-half earlier, in August 1961, and the city was still settling into its long and unhappy forced separation. There had been an exodus from West Berlin since the wall went up as life there became more constricted. Everywhere, it seemed, one ran up against the wall, and it was difficult to escape the feeling of being caged in.

We sublet a room in the only building left over from the war in a four-block area, at Friedrichstrasse 9, not far from Checkpoint Charlie in the working-class section of town known as Kreuzberg. Today this is again one of Berlin's more fashionable addresses. At that time it was a devastated urban landscape. In this part of Berlin there had been no reconstruction since the war. Our landlord was in jail for murder. His wife now lived there with her new lover and her daughter. As their electricity had been cut off for non-payment, they brazenly tapped into a neighbor's line and diverted some of the "juice" to us, their sub-tenants. The supply of coal from East Germany had been cut, so every day I had to scrounge through the dealerships in the neighborhood in the hopes of finding half a dozen or so charcoal briquettes to heat our tile stove, our only source of heat, which we also used to "cook" our food. Ingrid, at least, was able to obtain a job through the *Arbeitsamt*, the city employment agency. For me it was more difficult, despite the fact that I could claim German citizenship through Papa, thereby becoming eligible for rent-controlled housing. This later enabled me to get a room (a very run-down room, to be sure) for $6 a month (at an exchange rate of 4 DM to the dollar). Fritzi's daughter Andrea Kügelgen, who was living in Florence at the time but came to visit her mother in Berlin in December 1964, thought it was an amazing deal. She was paying ten times that much for a room of only marginally better quality.

We needed very little money to live in Berlin, which was a good thing, as money was precisely what we were lacking. Ingrid got a low-paying secretarial job, and I tried all sorts of expedients to earn money. A job that kept me in good shape physically, for a time, was distributing leaflets to every apartment in the four- or five-story tenements in the working-class borough of Wedding. I distributed leaflets from door to door for eight to ten marks a day, which immediately went for food and coal. I hurried up- and down-stairs and from building to building to get the feeling that I was earning a high hourly wage. At the start it always seemed as if it wouldn't take more than a couple of hours. But it was usually well into the afternoon before I had gotten rid of all one-thousand leaflets. I also worked as a day laborer, hiring myself out every morning to factories and businesses that needed temporary workers. My fellow job seekers were mostly in their late forties or fifties, too old or frail to get a permanent job. Many of them had been Communists before the war, and they could not understand how, as an educated member of the middle class, I could find myself in the same sorry state of unemployment as they. Eventually I did manage to make a half-way decent hourly wage in the time-honored expatriate occupation of teaching English at a local Berlitz-type school and giving German lessons to the large number of foreigners who came to Berlin, either as guest workers, or to study, or to seek political asylum under West Germany`s extremely liberal refugee policies.

Meanwhile I kept looking around for more remunerative employment. One ad in the *Berliner Morgenpost* seemed irresistible: "Leading American educational institution seeks educated gentlemen with fluent English as representatives." It turned out to be a job selling *Encyclopedia Britannica* to educated Germans, about which I wrote a short story that I couldn't get published. It was a psychological study of the man who hired me and stood to gain from every encyclopedia I sold (in three months I sold exactly one). He was a Greek immigrant by the name of Alexander who

> couldn't understand why I stayed in Berlin even though I was an American citizen and had my return ticket in my pocket. If he had a chance to go, he said, he'd go in a minute. He regarded it as unfair that I, who was so patently unqualified to make use of the opportunities there, should have access to America, while he did not. He asked me from what I lived. I told him I gave English lessons for four marks an hour. When I told him he could certainly give Greek lessons at the same school he screwed up his face, and I could see that he was spoiled for that kind of work for the rest of his life. I admit it is a funny feeling to chase after 270 marks all day (the commission for the sale of one set of encyclopedia) and then go and teach three exhausting hours in the evening for twelve marks.

> Alexander was unabashedly cynical: "The point is to get at other people's money. Not everyone can do it. It's a skill."

I also tried writing other stuff—that was, after all, my original intention in returning to Germany—but I was too exhausted from the daily grind, too weighed down by our hand-to-mouth existence, too out of touch with potential publishers, and too easily discouraged by rejection to produce anything of consequence. I thought I might follow George Orwell's example and write a book entitled, *Down and Out in Boston and Berlin.* For a time I thought I might try my hand at journalism, reporting on events in Berlin in *New Yorker* style, on the model of my cousin Christopher Rand's fascinating series of *New Yorker* articles on Salisbury, Connecticut, in the 1950s and early 1960s. As an American citizen I had no difficulty entering East Berlin, if I was willing to put up with the rather disagreeable "processing" at the border. Citizens of West Germany like Ingrid enjoyed this "privilege," too; only the citizens of West Berlin were barred from visiting their relatives and friends, as the Soviets tried to put pressure on the West to "normalize relations"—code language for granting diplomatic recognition to the East German regime and eventually incorporating all of Berlin into the German Democratic Republic.

Our first visit to the east was to the *Berolina Keller*, a Rathskeller on the Alexanderplatz, the square that gave its name to a famous expressionistic novel by Alfred Döblin in 1929 (and to a twelve-hour Hans Werner Fassbinder TV film in the 1970s).

> The Berolina Keller was full, smoky, and noisy, and a small "combo" was playing waltzes and "oompah" songs. There were so many young men in uniform that I thought at first it must be some sort of military club. But this was simply due to the fact that there aren't many drinking places in East Berlin whereas there *are* many soldiers. As we sat down at one of the long wooden tables, a matronly-looking middle-aged woman turned to us and said, "You're from the West, aren't you?" Since we had taken pains not to dress conspicuously, we wondered how she could tell so fast. "One can tell," she said...After a painful silence she turned to us and told us she had a son in West Germany. Since he had fled from East Berlin, he could not reenter without being arrested. Now that the wall had gone up there was no possibility of meeting in Berlin. She said she doubted that she would ever see him again. "The wall won't come down in our

lifetime," she said. Her home was in Thuringia, and she had come to East Berlin on her vacation. She found the East Berliners refreshing. "They rail against the party and against the wall here, and they don't care who hears them," she said. "Down where I live everyone's too scared."

Opposite us two young soldiers were sitting. It was interesting to note the suspicion with which the woman eyed them until she realized it was safe to speak in their company. They were so-called Grepos, short for *Grenzpolizei*—border police—and their duty was to patrol the wall and barbed wire against the escape attempts that occur almost daily. They showed the unmistakable signs of belonging to an unpopular organization. It was almost embarrassing to hear them apologize for their odious occupation. "The West Berliners have no right to shout 'pigs' and 'murderers' at us," one of them said. "We can't help that we have to be there. If we don't follow orders we get it worse than the people we keep from fleeing. Remember, we may have to shoot, but nobody can make us aim." We reminded him that nevertheless people were shot down at the wall at regular intervals. "Of course, there are some who aim. But at least eighty percent of the troops feel the way we do." I reflected what a powerful force contempt really was. It was what was gnawing away at the roots of this regime, and it is that, if anything, that will ultimately cause its change or its collapse. In all my future contacts with East Germans in any sort of official position, I was always struck by their almost touching desire to be liked.

In May 1963 we visited East Berlin to participate in a so-called *Deutschlandtreffen*, a youth rally (to which Westerners were also invited) staged by the regime to demonstrate its popular support.

After repeated visits to the East one gets used to the back-patting slogans displayed in 1984 fashion on banners and buildings—the same way one gets used to some of the preposterous commercial advertising in the West. The street signs which lined the Friedrichstrasse beyond Checkpoint Charlie—the crossing point for foreign visitors—would have been amusing if they hadn't been so militant. "Peace has the right of way," one sign read, and, "Closed to *revanchists*" or "Passing on the Left only," the latter a play on the German word "*überholen*," which also means "surpassing."

In front of the university on *Unter den Linden* and in front of the Brandenburger Tor organized discussions were taking place. Westerners, or Easterners speaking in opposition to the party line (mostly by posing provocative questions) were easy to identify: by their red faces and latent sweat—or by following the direction of everyone's eyes. Opposite each red-faced "Westerner" stood a pale, cool, suave Eastern functionary, some more, some less successful at retaining their artificial smiles over a long period of time. Around them a mob of mute young faces with fixed stares, showing no signs of approval or disapproval, as if they knew what to expect, but were interested in hearing it anyway—not listening to the arguments, but watching the drama.

The "discussions" made one admire the courage of the "Westerners," and their optimism in feeling that what they said did any good. Rarely have words seemed more useless or insufficient to me—less able to penetrate to the seat of conviction. Listening to the smooth, winning, rehearsed arguments of the party functionaries, I couldn't help thinking of what I had read somewhere: that the main fallacy of communism—what made it both impractical and unpopular—was that it was based on the "goodness" of man rather than on his natural egotism. It was this unrealistic assumption, this false idealism, that made communism so winning as a theory and so disappointing in practice. The supporters of communism could suck a kind of moral strength from their theory that was hard for opponents to combat without seeming to disown the goodness of man. Even the call for personal freedom seems immoral when it is opposed to "the good of the people."

One of the groups was different from the others. Here there was no "discussion." A man perhaps in his fifties was holding an address in the high-pitched manner of the soap-box speakers on Boston Commons on Sunday afternoons. It was an *Altkommunist*, a man who had been a member of the party before the war. These people, many of whom had been active in the resistance against the Nazis, are obviously accorded a good deal more respect, both in East and West, than those thousands who joined the party to further their careers after the war. "I am a worker," he was saying, "I am a locksmith. My two sons are studying at the university. Shouldn't I be pleased to be living in a state where this is possible?"

Around him a cluster of teenagers and youths, open-mouthed, politely nodded assent to the flurry of rhetorical questions directed at them.

Otherwise the streets were remarkably devoid of older people. There were even fewer than usual in the streets even though the regime had made a point of encouraging East Berliners to make the youngsters from the interior feel welcome and join in their celebration. This demonstration of public apathy seemed all the more significant in view of the fact that there were a number of generously staged outdoor concerts and shows, rare offerings in the otherwise rather drab entertainment fare in East Berlin. Only a handful of adults dotted the group of 150 to 200 youngsters who clustered around the giant stage on the steps of the city museum, where a Russian army chorus and dance troupe were performing with professional competence. Loudspeakers had been set up at distant points of the large square, and it was a strange sensation to hear the deep, full choral music blaring into the empty pavement.

Coming back across Checkpoint Charlie in the evening, an illuminated newscast flashing over from the West put a final damper on our visit. The broadcasting device (similar to the one on the Times Building in New York) had been mounted on the top of the highest building along the wall (by the publisher of West Germany's leading tabloid, the *Bild Zeitung*) and was facing to the East. It was flashing: "62,000 new homes were erected in the Federal Republic of Germany in 1963..." A number of curiosity-seeking youths had strayed from the centers of celebration to have a closer look at the newscast, but they obviously weren't much impressed. It occurred to me that this was precisely the sort of self-congratulatory propaganda that could only serve to strengthen the loyalty of East Germans to their regime. It reminded me of the Western "tourists" we had sometimes seen in the Berolina Keller, looking disdainfully at the obvious signs of poverty around them, and complaining about the poor quality of the beer.

It is, to be sure, not easy sometimes to hide the almost automatic condescension one feels for a society where not even cucumbers are available in sufficient quantities, not even soda water (because it is needed in the factories), where the roads are poor and the cars are few

> and burn lots of oil. These are symptoms of something wrong, no doubt, but a large proportion of Western visitors—and Easterners are sensitive to this—seem to regard these as the wrongs themselves. Even loyal East Germans are quite ready to admit the economic backwardness of their country—indeed how could they do otherwise—but they are not ready to admit this as a valid argument for the superiority of the Western way of life.

Ingrid and I split up later that year. She was not willing to continue living with me unless we got married, and this I was not willing to do after her traumatic *Seitensprung* with her ex-husband. "*Ich dachte es geht, aber es geht nicht*," she said laconically about living together unmarried (I thought it would work, but it won't). Thus jealousy and pride bore off the final triumph in our relationship. I was very aware of being the agent of my own unhappiness, but reason, of course, plays little role in such situations. In fact, I took a perverse satisfaction in my stubborn adherence to "principle." Emerson's notion of "character" (or of self-reliance as the essence of heroism) gave me the strength to persevere in the face of my natural inclinations. Sticking to principle was like hanging on to the strap or gripping a pole in a subway, I thought. It kept one from keeling over as the train lurched from side to side. Ingrid and I continued to see each other after our separation, however, and actually remained life-long friends.

My next sortie into East Berlin came in the company of Renate Sami, a colleague of mine who also taught English and German at the *Hartnackschule* in Berlin and would later make something of a name for herself as an independent experimental film maker. We visited Renate's first cousin, whose husband was a professor of botany at the University of Halle in the East German state of Sachsen-Anhalt and a member of the Communist Party (called Socialist Unity Party because it forcibly fused the Communist and Social Democratic parties).

Wit Ingrid at a dance in Berlin, 1963

Friedrich, a bright, capable man in his late thirties, has a "positive attitude" toward the state he is living in. Not that he considers everything that's done by the government as automatically right, but he *wants* his government to be right and is willing to help make it right. He is sensitive, of course, to the Western charge of lack of freedom, and sometimes he appeared to want to show us how critical of authority he could be. He inveighed against local police for their enforcement of a certain pointless traffic law in a way that was rather overdone.

Friedrich told us that the reason East Germany had such economic difficulties was its lack of natural resources. No mention of mismanagement, low worker morale, or the loss of manpower to the West. His rationalization for the wall showed a similar one-sidedness. "The West Berliners kept coming over and buying our goods because they could get them cheaper here. They had much more buying power than East Berliners because they simply stocked up on East currency at the Western rate of exchange, three to four East marks for one West mark (the Eastern rate of exchange was one to one)." I said there had been safeguards taken against this by making every purchaser in East Berlin show their identification card, so this could not have been the real reason for the wall. But Friedrich refused to admit that its primary purpose was to prevent the flow of refugees to the West. "Recognize us," he said, "and there will be free traffic between our countries."

Friedrich is in no sense a fanatic party member. One proof of this was that his friends, some of whom were a good deal more critical of the regime, felt no compunctions about speaking openly in front of him. The host of a small after-dinner party to which we were invited was a concert pianist. His mother was living in West Germany and kept him supplied with cigarettes and coffee through the mail. He made a good deal of fun at the regime in a harmless way—perhaps, I felt, to make us feel comfortable. What he couldn't stand, he said, was the condescending attitude many West Germans had toward the "German Democratic Republic." "Of course, the regime is oppressive and there's lots of mismanagement, but to think that there are no more intelligent people here at all is going too far."

I had brought my guitar along. Among the tunes I sang were loyalist songs from the Spanish Civil War, some of them in German, and *Wir sind die Moorsoldaten,* a song sung by political prisoners in Nazi concentration camps in the 1930s. Our host was quite astonished that I knew these songs and that they could be freely published and performed in the

West. He asked me whether I would be staying in Germany. I told him I would probably go back to America sooner or later. Asked whether I wanted to settle down there, I told him I didn't particularly want to stay put anywhere. "I wish we could say that," he said.

At our request Friedrich took us to visit the painter Albert Ebert, whose pictures, miniature-sized and primitive in style, have attained a certain success both in the East and—more important as a commentary on their artistic quality—in the West. We found him in front of his old stone house on the banks of the Saale River, preparing to have his morning beer (not his first, according to Friedrich). He greeted us with the wariness of a hunted animal, but after Friedrich's brash introduction (he introduced himself as an old acquaintance, although they had only met for one evening two years ago), he prepared to show us some of his works. His wife was likewise suspicious and more openly rude and forbade him to draw back the curtains lest the heat come in. So we looked at his miniatures by the light of a floor lamp and Friedrich's suave mixture of questions and compliments. Albert Ebert replied mostly yes or no; when he was called on for a longer answer, his voice reminded me of handwriting that dips toward the bottom at the end of each line. Then he showed us his studio. The smell of the oil paint separated it sharply from the other rooms in the house and made me think I understood why a man might be driven to painting.

Albert Ebert, who had quite warmed up to us by now, told us he would get into trouble if he sold paintings to persons from the West. He had already been called to account because so many of his paintings were to be found in West Germany now. He denied, however, selling his paintings to any but East German buyers. He couldn't help it, he told the party functionaries, if the people who bought his paintings fled to the West and took his paintings with them.

Our car, one of the tiny but precise West German makes, was a symbol of the wrong relations between East and West. Friedrich asked us to park it behind the house, where it couldn't be seen, not because people would suspect him of being pro-West, but because people would envy him for having visitors from the West. And when we went to call on people who did not expect us—such as Albert Ebert—Friedrich considerately had us leave the car at some distance from the house so as not to unduly startle the persons we were going to see.

Friedrich's attitude toward the West, for all its competitiveness and defensiveness, has also a wistful quality, a regret at being outside the mainstream of the world's activity and attention. He pored over the Western newspapers we managed to sneak through the border controls. The political news helped him to see the point behind East German political maneuvers and policies, he said, and he thought East German papers might do the same for us. He told us about a research trip he would be taking to North Vietnam in the fall. With some pride he told us about the Aeroflot jetliner that would be carrying him from Moscow to Peking in a matter of a few hours.

Both Friedrich and his wife Rosel are greatly interested in music. With many distinguished Russian guest performers, it is one area where the East can very well hold its own with the West. But more importantly, music lies outside the main arena of competition, and one has the feeling that all of the East Germans' day-by-day preoccupations lie very much within this arena. The attempts to whip up a sense of national mission—such as through huge signs proclaiming socialism as Germany's future—have pretty feeble results, but the intra-German rivalry does have a mobilizing function. The West German level is the standard to which East Germans aspire in all fields, just as the U. S. level is the standard to which the Soviet Union aspires. This summer of East-West athletic competition to determine the all-German Olympic team has given the East-West rivalry a ready outlet. Particularly Andreas, the 14-year-old eldest son, was elated over an unexpected East German field hockey victory on the weekend we were there.

Rosel is guided by her devotion to her husband. She shares his political attitude, but gives the distinct impression that she would never have arrived at this point of view if it weren't for him. Her attitude bespeaks loyalty, not conviction. At breakfast on the day we drove back to West Berlin, she said that she wished she could come along. She turned to her

> son Andreas and asked him whether he would come too, if he could, but he proudly shook his head.

Andreas grew up to earn a doctorate in zoology and eventually became the director of the city zoo in Halle. In that capacity he actually survived the transition to a united Germany in 1990. At the time there were those who sought to oust him because of his party membership, an affiliation which now redounded to his disadvantage. Nonetheless, his irreproachable professional credentials and the at least nominally non-political nature of his job enabled him to hold on to his position. But he never forgave Gorbachev for what he thought was an irresponsible surrender of power to the West.

I was in Berlin on 26 June 1963, when President Kennedy made his famous speech. For years thereafter I had to assure my American friends that he hadn't actually told the crowd he was a Berlin pastry. Of course, he should have said "*Ich bin Berliner*," rather than "*Ich bin ein Berliner*" (a "Berliner" being a particular form of pastry), but nonetheless, it took more than a little ill will to so deliberately distort his meaning. I was not among the over 100,000 people who actually attended his speech at the *Schöneberger Rathaus*, the city hall of the neighboring borough of Schöneberg. But I do remember listening to it on the radio and taking considerable pride in our charismatic young president.

Meanwhile, I came under the baneful influence of a new and startling addiction: the game of chess. Chess was an obvious escape mechanism—an excuse to procrastinate—yet this function made its hold over me all the fiercer. It is no exaggeration to say that chess became my number one priority, taking precedence over such purposeful activities as writing or all other more conventional forms of socializing. I began playing chess in the city parks just to while away the time and to get the cheap kicks of winning. I found that the game came back quickly to me, and that with a little work and preparation I could do quite well against the limited competition I faced. Then I began in a desultory way to study the game, checking out books from the library and playing over games by myself for hours on end. I began to really understand the game and found considerable gratification in planning strategies to entrap my opponents. I joined a club, the venerable *Schachclub Kreuzberg*, today one of the leading clubs in Germany's *Bundesliga*, the nation's top chess league, with a star-studded lineup of international grandmasters. It didn't help that in those days the club met in a café on the Yorckstrasse, just across the square from where I lived on Gneisenaustrasse 4. Later the club moved to the Moritzplatz, forcing me to ride a couple of stops on the subway, and today it owns a building of its own. At the *Schachclub Kreuzberg* I met older men who had literally wasted their lives on chess. Rudolf Elstner and Adolf Pawelczak come to mind, both expert players who died in utter poverty in their late 60s or early 70s in 1966, never having done anything else in their lives but play and write about chess. But chess is a young man's game, and I benefitted from youth and the stamina this gave me. I had no natural talent for chess, as Olaf had, with his mathematical mind. All of the success I enjoyed was by dint of hard work that would have been far better spent on writing. I started off on one of the lower-ranking club teams, but by 1965 I was playing on the top team, on the third or fourth boards. My name is still carried on the club rolls today as the winner of the club championship in 1965 and runner-up in 1966.

I saw through the cheap thrills that the game conferred, but could not resist its lure. On 19 July 1963 I registered my ambivalence in my journal:

> How disappointing the chess club here is! Greedy, win-crazed players who spoil one's appetite for the game. The way they slam the pieces around to cow and impress their opponent is symptomatic of their attitudes. I despise weaklings who glorify "good sportsmanship" and "good losers" and devalue winning because they do it so rarely—who turn losing into "winning" so that they may emerge as winners after all—these are the backside of the same coin. How I enjoy the players who love the game and to whom winning is simply one of the essential principles that make up the game. The opponent who is really a partner in a joint and delicious enterprise.

I continued my journal to the point where I diagnosed myself as suffering from "diarytis," "the ultimate in diary-sickness, revising, editing, improving previous entries." Many of my entries were about writing itself, as in this entry more than a year after Marilyn Monroe's suicide in August 1962:

> Joe Dimaggio suing Arthur Miller for "intellectual exhibitionism!" Poor Albert (Lotte's husband in *The Sorrows of Young Werther*) could have sued Goethe, too. And how many could have sued Proust! Didn't Sinclair Lewis call writing (or at least his writing, the motive for it) itself "intellectual exhibitionism?" According to that definition Arthur Miller is being sued

> for writing. But it's an interesting gesture on the part of Dimaggio. It is no mean accomplishment to get a writer to admit what he's doing. Or to get him to tell a lie. In either case M.M. is avenged.

My formal writing suffered from inexcusable neglect, but I did do a lot of reading when I wasn't preoccupied with chess. Of course I devoured the Berlin stories of Christopher Isherwood and from there went on to read all his novels, including his works on Vedanta. I also read the undeservedly neglected series of novels by Anthony Powell, "Dance to the Music of Time," and Lawrence Durrell's "Alexandria Quartet." My political education began with Edmund Wilson's *To the Finland Station*, a book I found immensely moving, which encouraged me to continue with his very entertaining *Memoirs of Hecate County. Berlin Alexanderplatz* was the German novel that made the greatest impression on me. I read it while lying on the bed next to Ingrid, and when Biberkopf's girlfriend was killed by his best friend in a classic double-cross in Berlin's criminal underworld, I had to do real violence to myself to fight back the tears. Later I wondered whether our relationship might not have taken a much more positive turn if I had just given in to my overwhelming urge to cry.

I was playing a pick-up game at the chess club in the evening of 22 November 1963, when the announcement came through that President Kennedy had been shot in Dallas. There was a stunned silence in the hall, and I promptly made what turned out to be the losing move in my game. Kennedy's assassination seemed to me to be a real turning point, and I looked to the future with foreboding. To me Lyndon B. Johnson represented a different direction in American politics from the liberal Kennedy administration. Common sense might have suggested that in fact the change would not be nearly so great as it seemed to me at the time. After all, it was LBJ who brought to fruition the civil rights legislation that might never have passed if Kennedy had remained in office. It was LBJ who sponsored the Great Society legislation that included, among other things, the introduction of Medicare and Medicaid. My more radical friends could never understand what they thought was my totally unwarranted veneration of Kennedy's supposedly more left-wing credentials. Years later, for instance, Bart Bernstein of Stanford, visiting Spokane for a guest lecture, contradicted my claim that American policy in Vietnam would have been different under Kennedy than it was under Johnson—after all, "the best and the brightest" continued to serve under Johnson. This was not my sense, however, and I remember in the election of 1964 taking little comfort from the fact that LBJ was way ahead in the polls. My brother Olaf misattributed my concern to fear that Johnson might lose to Goldwater and told me I needn't worry. But I wasn't worried about that at all: I was worried that things couldn't help but get worse no matter who won the election. In the event my instincts turned out to be right.

In early May 1964 the Stackelberg family organization celebrated the 100th anniversary of its incorporation under the statutes of the Russian Empire in 1864. I had several close Stackelberg relatives living in Berlin. My great-aunt Tatjana (1891-1970), the ethnic Russian widow of my great-uncle Berndt (1882-1960), invited me to her periodic Sunday dinners, sumptuous feasts at which the vodka flowed liberally.

Tante Tatjana at home in the late 1960s

Members of Berlin's small Russian Orthodox community were also frequently invited, and Russian was the language of choice at these meals, although due consideration was taken of those of us of the younger generation, which included Tatjana's grandchildren Angelika (Geli) and Herrmann Lutz, who did not speak the language. Their older brother Peter Lutz, a pilot in the *Bundeswehr*, was eventually adopted by TanteTatjana and officially integrated into the Stackelberg genealogy. At Tante Tatjana's I met Tschutscheff, an elderly veteran of the *Baltenregiment*, a military force organized by the Baltic aristocracy to fight against the Bolsheviks in 1918-1919. They were all fierce anti-communists with more than just a touch of the anti-Semitism that was so typical of the monarchist side in the Russian civil war. Tatjana's daughter Marina Lutz (1911-1997), the paid director of the local Berlin bridge club and a championship player herself, had never gotten along with my mother, as she freely confessed to me. Once, during the war, according to her account, Mama and Wini had taken her food ration stamps, even though they had invited her to dinner. But worse, they had made fun of her in a way that obviously still grated on her after all these years. I could indeed imagine what remorseless fun Mama and Wini must have had at her expense.

Despite the liability of my maternal descent (and the dangerously liberal politics that could no doubt be traced to this source), I was welcomed at these dinners as my father's son. Tante Tatjana was used to living beyond her very limited means, and Papa was a ready source of funds. Whenever Tatjana went on vacation, she would announce this fact to my father, knowing that she could count on him to send her a few hundred marks. "In financial matters she is totally without scruples," Papa warned me. "She often telegraphs me from Spain, 'Coming Saturday, have 200 marks ready,' or 'Train is passing through Karlsruhe at night, can't visit, please send 200 marks.'" Under the mistaken impression that I was getting an allowance from Papa, she tried to borrow money from me. Papa advised me to tell her that lightning had struck my account. "She'll understand." But Papa was grateful to Tante Tatjana for holding the family together in Berlin, and I was the beneficiary of the enormous admiration she had for Papa. So great was the glory that reflected on me through her eyes that she was sure I was the tallest of all her dinner guests even though I was at least an inch or two shorter than some of the others. She also thought I had the best handwriting, a judgment that was manifestly wrong.

With my second cousin Angelika I attended the family's 100th anniversary celebration at *Schloß Kronberg* in the Taunus, close to Frankfurt. Among the attendees there were a handful of septuagenarian Stackelbergs who had participated in the grand 50th anniversary *Familientag* in Tallinn (known to us by its German name of Reval) in May 1914 on the eve of the First World War. A small number of participants at the 75th anniversary celebration in Reval in 1939 were also present, the last family get-together before the expulsion of Baltic Germans from Estonia in the wake of the Nazi-Soviet Pact on the eve of the Second World War. We set off for Frankfurt by train on May 1st, a holiday in the GDR. People waiting to cross the tracks waved to us, quite different from our return trip four days later, a working day, when nobody responded to my waves. One of the highlights of the weekend was doing the twist with Angelika at the formal Saturday evening ball. The champagne and the music unleashed that wild rhythmic frenzy in me that usually embarrassed even Ingrid in the *Tanzkneipen*. So I did my best to control it and this touch of restraint must have looked good because we were applauded at the end. Angelika curtseyed and I bowed.

As is often the case at such functions, the only really unconstrained, almost familial atmosphere came at the leave-taking at the end. "Just beginning," I wrote in my journal, "in saying goodbye, to get to know those two or three persons you really want to get to know."

> Karl-August made the best speech, with such wonderful ideas, one despairs of anyone taking them seriously, even he who professes them. Like those who admire existential values, but don't live according to them. It was a speech addressed to the youth, and urged *Bescheidenheit* (modesty), and: *"Geht eure eigenen Wege. Ihr müsst den Mut zum selbständigen Denken haben"* (go your own paths, you have to have the courage for independent thinking.)

Most of the older generation, I thought, showed little interest in getting to know the younger generation better. It seemed to be more important to find out what they "did." Not surprisingly, that put me at a considerable disadvantage to others of my age. Steno, the family genealogist who had lived in Washington, DC, since before the war, seemed disappointed that I did not fit the image of the American(ized) Stackelbergs he had presented in his talk. Under the pretext of seeking an ashtray he literally wound himself out of a conversation in which I thought I had perhaps taken Onkel Ernie`s instructions to use the "du" in the family a bit too seriously. I missed Tempy, with whom I had attended a number of *Baltenbälle*, the first one in Stuttgart back in early 1959. Without Tempy it was harder to extract humor from the situation. I don`t know that Papa`s *Damenrede*, a panegyric to the ladies meant to be amusing, was much different from the one he held in Stuttgart, but I found the earlier one incomparably funnier. My eyes and ears had lost the sense of the comic in his appearance, deportment, and delivery.

Familienfest at Schloß Kronberg, May 1964, with Wolfhart, who succeeded Papa as president of the family organization, at the head of the table

This time there were

> no drinks in the bar with Onkel Ernie. No laughter and joking with Onkel Ernie. Only, *"Du bist jetzt Journalist, oder was?"* dry-serious, over a meal he invited himself to at Papa`s table. Papa quickly explained that I was writing a book, and would perhaps write a whole series, like Balzac.

I did value the opportunity to get to make the acquaintance of Traugott, a wonderfully sensitive writer and the most famous living Stackelberg at the time. In the First World War he had been deported to Siberia as one of the Baltic Germans whose loyalty to the Russian monarchy was in doubt. He was not released until after the overthrow of the czar in 1918. I would have loved to have talked to him about his experiences and his politics. But, quite understandably, Traugott took no notice of me, lavishing his attentions instead on Angelika, who enjoyed the *Fest* immensely and despaired of ever being able to tell Tante Tatjana how wonderful everything had been. At the banquet my *Tischdame* (dinner partner), who had married a Frenchman and was now living in Paris, politely claimed she envied me for living in Berlin: "*Da ist doch Spannung*" (there`s tension there.)

Our lengthy departure at the end drew the ire of a "*Wirtschaftsbonze*" (economic boss) who honked the horn of his huge Mercedes, showing his annoyance at being blocked from the hotel entrance by such an ill-assorted and impecunious group. Apparently we didn`t have the grace to leave and make room for the next (and wealthier) set of guests. When the bellboy explained who we were and what function we were attending, the *Bonze* broke into a loud fit of laughter. Encouraged by this (and no doubt speculating on a large tip), the bellboy unabashedly joined in. But there was a nice article about us in the paper. It spoke of the "worn shiny black of the tuxedos throwing the pallor of their faces into relief" and of the "distant look in their eyes, toward the homeland they will never see again." No one at that time could have foreseen that the 125th anniversary reunion in 1989 would once again be held in Tallinn.

9
Goodbye to Berlin, 1965-1967

I met Steffi Heuss in February 1965 at a party thrown by one of the younger members of the Bismarck family studying in Berlin, to which I was invited through my Baltic connections. Steffi and I almost didn't meet. I was on my way out the door, disappointed as usual, when she caught my eye. I could tell immediately she was not like anyone else I had ever met. I thought the German word *burschikos* described her well, a term only inadequately translated as "tomboyish." She obviously had a mind of her own. I was attracted to her informality and fascinated by what seemed to me her genuine indifference to the conventions of the "high" society in which she, by accident, found herself.

She didn't seem to give a hoot what I thought of her, and it was precisely this trait that made me stay for just one more dance. I was intrigued at the way she immediately assumed the male role, swinging me around the dance floor with abandon. She later confessed that she had done this as a deliberate provocation, a protest against the maddening enervation of most of the young men she had met at the party. It seemed she was demonstrating the way we men should be conducting ourselves, with energy and decisiveness. I actually found the idea that she might just be toying with men for her own amusement quite exciting. Of course, a strong woman was exactly what I needed to help me break out of my doldrums. In the months to come she gave me emotional security, a feeling of being loved and wanted, and a new-found sense of confidence. We couldn't get enough of each other during those first few weeks, sometimes staying up all night, talking and making love. Steffi put it well: "It was as if we hadn't seen each other for a long time."

It was sobering to realize how fortuitous our meeting had been. Not only had I met her while fully determined to leave the party, but it turned out that she, too, was there only by virtue of a last-minute decision to accompany a friend. Such fortuity reinforced my sense that we were meant for each other. I got the same feeling a few weeks later when entirely by chance I entered the very same subway car in which Steffi was sitting. Contributing to our mutual attraction, to be sure, was the fact that we were both on the rebound: I from Ingrid, and Steffi from her boyfriend Gundi, a colleague of hers trained at the same goldsmith school in Schwäbisch-Gmünd in the state of Baden-Württemberg where she had earned her diploma as well, certifying her mastery of the craft. When I met her she was still full of resentment against Gundi for ending their long-term relationship. But for me their break-up was a godsend, and I was quite willing to be the vehicle of her revenge. Steffi gave my life a direction and a purpose. I shudder to think what would (not) have become of me if she had abandoned our tentative attempt to make a life together, as I occasionally feared she would, especially at the outset of our relationship, when she still left taunting notes on Gundi`s windshield whenever she saw his car parked in the neighborhood. But end up together we did, to the considerable surprise of some of my friends. Olaf Meyer, one of my theologian friends from Heidelberg who was now studying in Berlin (where he would later take over one of the Lutheran parishes), was amazed I had it in me to make such a redoubtable and attractive conquest.

"Our living together on such short notice," I wrote in my journal, "was an acceptance at first sight, a trust in advance, like buying a car on impulse without knowing whether it works. What glorious pleasure then, when it functions smoothly!" From the beginning it was understood that we would live together, but not bother to get married unless our union produced a child, a possibility to which neither of us was averse. I was going to be 30 that year, and while men may not have the same "biological clock" as women, there is no doubt that men do have a mating urge that—inversely to the sexual urge—increases with age (I still remember Ken Baldridge telling me, "I decided, come what may, I would be married by the time I was 35"). Steffi, who turned 24 in February 1965, not only had no objections to living together in the meantime; she actually preferred the unmarried state, partly to demonstrate her freedom from convention, but mainly to preserve her independence. She was herself the product of a broken marriage. After their bitter divorce her parents refused to talk to each other for the rest of their lives, a pattern Steffi was determined not to repeat.

Neither physically, nor intellectually, was I the type of person she had expected to end up with, but things certainly worked out well for a time. Once on one of our walks, she pointed to the picture of a handsome man (was it the "Marlboro man"?) on an advertising billboard: "That's my type. So independent." To me it seemed as if he were caught in a spider's web of interdependence and commitments—to business, parents, friends, social opinion, possessions, not to mention tobacco (to which Steffi also was addicted). Steffi said that the animal I most resembled was a deer: in body build, shyness, nervousness, distrust and dislike of people, love of solitude, pacifism, defenselessness and helplessness, but also agility. Self-deprecatingly, she compared herself to a wild boar, stubbornly running up against everything and everybody, but herbivorous, not carnivorous. But she also thought of herself as "soft," easily swayed by firm opinions. One of her most appealing traits in my eyes was her admission that she tried to adopt opinions she thought I would approve of. Yet she criticized me for my adamant opposition to the Vietnam War. "Do you always have to oppose majority opinion?" She wanted me to be respectable so that she could be as proud of me as she would have been if I had indeed been professionally successful.

We complemented each other in a way that reflected to her advantage. While I spent most of my energies on unproductive *grübeln* (brooding) in my futile efforts to write, Steffi was a person of action, impulsive and spontaneous, frequently changing her mind, to be sure, but someone who could make decisions and get things done. In May, largely on her initiative, we moved to the Möckernstrasse in Kreuzberg into the shed of an old industrial building in the *Hinterhof* of a *Neubau*. The owner, Herr Bromberger, was planning to convert this pre-war industrial shed into a garage for his newly-finished apartment building, but as construction would be delayed for financial reasons until mid-1967, he was anxious to rent out the idle space in the interim. For us it was perfect: lots of room (on two floors), inexpensive, isolated from the residential portion of the building, the ideal setting for an unconventional household that would include both our living quarters and Steffi's jewelry *Werkstatt*. The fact that we would have to move out in two years was a slight drawback but would have the advantage of forcing us to make up our minds where to spend and what to do with the rest of our lives.

With Steffi in our Möckernstraße quarters, 1965

For Steffi the question of what she was going do with her life was completely settled. She was determined to design and make jewelry, a craft for which she had great talent and great love. She also had considerable success whenever her jewelry could be exposed to the view of potential customers. Marketing was definitely her weak suit, as it was mine as well. This fact was not lost on her two-years-younger sister Ulrike and her *geschäftstüchtige* (business-savvy) 46-year-old partner Arturo, a *Kunstschmied* who made fancy metal door handles, name-plates, and the like. Ulrike and Arturo lived in Munich, where Arturo made an excellent living. He also turned out *Schmuckstücke* (handcrafted jewelry), simply for ready cash, he said. He sold them to tourists and other buyers at a stand on the Leopoldstrasse, taking advantage of its heavy pedestrian traffic. He offered to sell Steffi's pieces there, too, on consignment, and for that purpose she had sent some samples to Munich months before. She did not receive the orders she had hoped for, but Arturo did pay her the compliment of imitation, mass-reproducing her beautiful original designs.

This was a problem Steffi would face throughout her career. I was impressed by the way she dealt with this kind of "plagiarism:"

> Steffi`s reaction was exemplary. As she had already done in school whenever classmates copied her models, she simply turned to something new. She could not compete with Arturo in manual dexterity, but in the variety and originality of her ideas she far outdistanced him. If he continued to copy her, he would have to see and admit to himself what he was doing. It is a better method than complaining or even than setting up copyright laws.

For the discriminating eye Steffi`s handiwork would continue to be unique.

Photo by Ulrike, June 1965

Ulrike and Arturo were among our first visitors at our pad in the backyard at Möckernstrasse 114, arriving in their late-model American car in late May 1965 and staying for several days. Apparently they were delegated by Steffi's mother and step-father to examine and report on Steffi's new boyfriend. "Finally," was the first thing Ulrike said when I came back from work, "*wir sind schon ganz gespannt* (we are very much in suspense)." The unspoken rivalry between the two sisters was fascinating to observe. Ulrike's self-esteem was based on her expectation that Steffi needed help in practical matters. All her life her sobriety and reasonableness had been there to guide her more exuberant older sister through the practical side of life. She immediately set about refashioning Steffi's workshop, ordering Arturo to build her a table, some shelves, and other useful accessories. Saturday afternoon Ulrike brought a huge pile of groceries and other household items and deposited them on the sofa. "*So. Pack mal aus*," she said to Steffi, who, if she heard her request, gave no indication of it. I unpacked the things in a matter-of-fact way, not expressing the level of gratitude that Ulrike apparently expected.

"*Wir sind uns fremd geworden* (we have become strangers)," was Steffi's summation of her reunion with her sister. "She now has Arturo to whom she tells everything, and she doesn't need me anymore." Some of Arturo's comments revealed that he was comparing the two sisters with a view to justifying his own lot. "Even though she's two years younger," he told me, "Ulrike is in a way much older than Steffi. She lives her life much more consciously." I hastened to agree with him, pleased that he could so easily persuade himself, and pleased that I could so readily see through his rationalization. According to Steffi's mother, however, they were more generous in their appraisal of our relationship than we had expected. We made an excellent couple, they said, and suited each other like hand in glove. The one thing they couldn't understand, they said, was our lack of ambition, by which they meant our apparent willingness to rough it and live in poverty. Steffi didn't demand enough of me, they said; and they themselves had tried to animate Steffi to greater activity. "*So gute Menschen wie wir findet ihr nie* (you'll never find such good people as us)," Ulrike said, referring to their offer to sell Steffi's work at their stand on the Leopoldstrasse. However, not only did this outlet never provide a reliable source of income for us, but a year later Ulrike was forced by her break-up with Arturo to borrow a substantial sum from her sister.

Steffi's sketches on the wall at Möckernstraße

We had another guest that summer, whom we came to refer to (among ourselves) as the *Kauz* (oddball). His visit led to the following entry in my journal on 21 June 1965:

> With a sigh of relief we saw our anonymous weekend guest off yesterday evening. The *Baltische Jugendgruppe* held a *Tagung* in Berlin and had asked its members to make sleeping space available for participants. I had offered the use of our sofa because Steffi said we should do so. Later she claimed she had said this only to please me. This is one of her foibles which I have come to accept. (When we moved in she said she had made the curtains only for me. She would never have made them for herself.) I knew she loved to meet "new people" and was sorry that I didn`t cultivate my ties to my Baltic compatriots.
>
> I myself had misgivings from the start. It was not that I expected an unpleasant person; it was rather that I didn`t think we could offer the comfort and freedom of movement he might expect. So it was with relief that I heard he was only 23 and without a *Beruf* (vocation) and that he had flunked his *Abitur*. This gave promise of a Tempy-like nature, easy-

going, open-minded, unassuming, enterprising, and fun to have around. It wasn`t long before I realized my mistake.

One must, of course, make allowance for the shock that people who don`t expect anything unusual get when exposed to Steffi`s *Werkstatt* and our way of life. I remember the excitement of Steffi`s screaming designs when I first saw them, but I also remember finding it offensively ostentatious to plaster them on the walls. I felt an involuntary resistance to her gradual take-over of the walls in my Gneisenaustrasse place. Even now, when I become aware of it, the design with the lettering *"C'est moi, que j'aime la vie"* in the *Werkstatt* strikes a chord of irritation in me, but I am hardly ever aware of it anymore. Visitors are, however, though I tend to forget this. Either they feel inhibited, or more generally, challenged or even affronted.

"I like living this way," our visitor assured us, running his eyes around the *Werkstatt.* "I'm not at all for great comfort. I place much more value on personal expression." He asked whether it was hard to get in to the art academy here. He planned to come to Berlin, study art, and get his *Abitur* on the side. His plans changed quite often, as we found out in the course of the weekend. At one point, impressed by my hourly wage (exaggerated by Steffi) and the low number of hours I worked, he told Steffi he wanted to become a teacher. It shouldn't be hard to pick up the necessary training, and he could always put up with some Baltic family until he found a place of his own. Steffi called him a bouncing ball.

Conversation with him was impossibly tedious. He was equipped with ready-made opinions on every subject, and delivered them in an aggravatingly obtrusive manner. I thought it was his east-German [Saxon] accent and elocution that reminded me so much of that arch-schoolmaster, my boss Lauterbach, until I realized it was his entire manner. Like Herr Lauterbach he had that annoying manner of forcing one to pay attention to him or else be rude. Seeing the listener in discomfort only egged him on. This is a form of paranoia, too: not to be satisfied until people are angry at you. This symptom wasn't restricted to his conversation. As soon as he saw we would rather be alone, he kept hanging around. He was continually getting detached from his group, either because he came too late or because he went to the wrong place. The most telling incident occurred Saturday afternoon: coming out of Aschingers with members of his group, he remembered he had forgotten his umbrella. By the time he had run back and fetched it the group had disappeared around a corner, and he wasn't able to find them again.

As I had no intention of being provoked into rudeness, I avoided every direct confrontation with him under the motto "live and let live." Only once, on the last day, I couldn't resist a sarcastic remark. We had been discussing the pros and cons of sitting with one's back to the window. I said it was much more pleasant (in class, for instance) not to look directly into the light. After all, one doesn't take pictures against the light, either. "One can take very good pictures against the light," our guest contradicted. "I always do. It produces very interesting pictures."—"Well, you always do extraordinary things," I said, but immediately realized he had won a small victory. Steffi's method was much more effective, because less premeditated. She broke out into a fit of laughter during one of his lecture-sermons. He stopped abruptly and got red. It dawned on me that he absolutely couldn't help the way he was.

Perhaps the most irritating thing was that one couldn't pin any palpable fault on him. He made one feel uncomfortable, but could one blame him if he didn't do so deliberately? I found myself getting increasingly insecure, not wanting to listen, but feeling foolish for not wanting to, feeling bullied, but feeling foolish for feeling so. It went so far that I even caught myself falling into his manner. It seemed to me at times that I had caught his complexes. It was like being infected by the patient one is treating. I was terribly worn out after this weekend, not so much from fighting with him as from sharing his troubles vicariously. I hardly slept the first night, thinking that our guest downstairs couldn't possibly feel comfortable. He certainly was on edge. Half an hour after going to bed he gave a terrible scream (or did I dream it?). He had mistaken his suit hanging by the window for a burglar. In the morning we found curtain and curtain rod torn down lying on the floor. He excused himself with a long drawn-out tale of how he had foiled a burglar in a vacation bungalow the year before.

At times I thought to my horror that I recognized myself in him. Certainly his compulsive talking cloaked a desperate shyness. How often have I said inanities, empty slogans, anything, just so as not to be excluded from the conversation? How often have I talked myself into mental equilibrium, but felt lost again as soon as I stopped? How often have I cemented my confidence with the authority of my statements, with the incontrovertibility of my convictions?

As far as paving the way to the personal connections we had hoped for, our guest was useless. I'm sure he is regarded rather askance by his fellow-Baltics, although this wasn't evident at the Saturday evening dance to which Steffi and I also went. His "type" is very "popular" at such affairs because of the surplus of girls who need a dancing partner, any dancing partner. I thought I detected furtive glances in our direction to make sure we were watching each time he spun a new partner around the floor. He didn't once come over to us all evening, and even this struck me as a form of showing off. It was as if to say, see how busy I am, I have no time for you, or, see how well I can get along without you? It never occurred to me that this was a breach of etiquette as well. He reminded us of this the next day by apologizing with obvious relish at the offence of not having danced with Steffi.

And how did we appear to him? As an unholy alliance maliciously out to bait him or put him on his mettle? As a closed and impenetrable society of two?

Income was a problem for us, of course, and became an even more urgent problem later that summer when Steffi got pregnant. I steadily increased the hours that I worked until the birth of our baby in April 1966, when I began working full time for the *Hartnackschule*. This was a language school that had enjoyed considerable renown for the quality of its instruction before the war, but seemed quite old-fashioned in the 1960s. It was run by the 60-year old Herr Lauterbach, a caricature of the German schoolmaster type. Like Ken Baldridge, he was an entrepreneur intent on making a profit; but unlike Baldridge, Lauterbach was (as I wrote in my journal) "inhibited by deep-seated traditions and pedagogical certainties." When I first joined the staff in 1963 the school was still using an antiquated and stilted prewar text in its English classes. Most of its classes were offered on the school's premises in a grand old building that had survived the war near the centrally-located Nollendorfplatz. But Lauterbach also contracted with firms to provide instructors for classes on site. On one of these assignments I traveled twice a week to the *Reemtsma* cigarette factory (turning out the *Peter Stuyvesant* brand on an impressive high-speed assembly line), which had recently been acquired by a British tobacco firm. English lessons were supposed to help the German management communicate with their British colleagues and read the literature sent to them by the head office in London. The text I was asked to use in my class was the monthly tobacco industry trade journal published in London. But I made the mistake of selecting an article that reported the ongoing research on the risks of cancer and provided arguments to counter the charge that smoking was linked to a higher incidence of disease. The article generated considerable interest among the staff, but also a visibly growing discomfiture on the part of the top managers, who evidently would have preferred to address a different topic. The English class, always conducted in a haze of smoke, soon lost some of its more prominent members. There was considerable pressure to smoke at the factory, and as a non-smoker I never really fit in, either. At any rate, the following year the contract for my services was not renewed.

For a time I also taught English grammar to American soldiers at McNair Barracks in Lichterfelde, as well as an early-morning class at the (now defunct) *Telefunken* headquarters on the Ernst Reuter Platz. Among my private students were a number of executives, such as the head of the Berlin branch of the Swiss *Sarotti* chocolate corporation. I also did an occasional stint as an interpreter, although I did not feel comfortable in this capacity. Having learned English and German separately from birth as my two native languages, I often had more difficulty finding the exact lingual equivalent than persons who had learned their German (or their English) in school. Much easier for me was written translation, which gave me more time to find the right word or phrase and the chance to use a dictionary if and when I got stuck. As it happened, Steffi's elderly cousin on her mother's side, Lilla Neumayer, born around the turn of the century, was one of the official translators of documents in *Wiedergutmachungs* (restitution) cases for victims of Nazism, Holocaust survivors, and their relatives. Tante Lilla steered much of this work to me, so I gained another fairly remunerative source of income. There was a note of tragedy in Tante Lilla's own biography. According to her account, her Jewish mother had exacted a deathbed promise from Tante Lilla and her siblings not to have children in order to spare them the persecution to which they would have been subjected as racial *Mischlinge* in Nazi Germany. In consequence Tante Lilla had never married, and she regretted never having the children she had wanted, to continue the family line and help alleviate the loneliness of her old age.

In late August 1965 Steffi and I traveled to Hamburg and Bremerhaven to meet Olaf and Cora and their three rambunctious boys, John, Peter, and Paul (born 1962) at the ocean liner that brought them to Germany for a sabbatical leave. Olaf had been awarded a year-long *Alexander von Humboldt* fellowship to do research and teach at Tübingen University near Stuttgart. He had already completed his third year of teaching at Duke University and was well on his way to an outstanding career in mathematics. Our reunion was cordial enough, but we soon found out that we disagreed about the Vietnam War. A year later when he and Cora visited Berlin on a Humboldt-sponsored tour, we even got into a heated argument about it. Olaf cited a letter from Mama in which she had said (in defense of U.S. intervention in Vietnam): "You have to remember that America has been a moral power for a century." Mama was not going to make the same mistake she made before the Second World War, when she found herself out of step with the official policy of her native country. Olaf made a much more materialistic argument as well, at one point asking "What about the natural resources of Southeast Asia? Are we just going to give them up?" a comment he later regretted. I actually found Cora's way of arguing more difficult to meet. "Do you think young American soldiers want to die in Vietnam?" she challenged me. I was flustered by this gross reframing of the debate. Only later I came up with the answer I wished I had given. "No, I think they'd much rather kill."

My opposition to the Vietnam War reflected and reinforced an almost irrational level of antagonism and hostility to the views of official America, so faithfully echoed by Olaf and Cora at the time. I wondered whether Mama's prediction that Olaf would turn Republican had in fact come true; after all, on this issue, he did not have to change parties to become a "Republican." Olaf in turn accused me, with considerable justification, of just "sitting in Berlin and criticizing." My radicalization had already proceeded to such an extent by then that I felt totally unshakeable in my views. I took comfort in knowing that even though I might not persuade Olaf and Cora to my view—might even "lose" the debate—there was no way that they could get me to change my mind. However, I also came to realize that the vehemence of my opposition did not help the anti-war cause. It only provoked contradiction, even among potential sympathizers. Apparently that was the effect I had on Cora, who later told Bridge, "I don't mind Tempy arguing against the war in Vietnam, but when Lodi does it I get really mad." Perhaps this was because I opposed the war on moral grounds, whereas Tempy opposed it on the more conservative grounds of realism and self-interest. He recognized that the war could not be won, except, as General LeMay advocated, by bombing Vietnam "back to the stone age."

The following year, back in America, Olaf chided me: "The first thing you do in a political argument is de-radicalize all around you so that you are then the most radical." However, on 4 August 1965 I had written in my journal:

> I can forgive America her Vietnam policy when I hear the news on AFN [Armed Forces Network]: no attempt to conceal the killing of civilians. A reporting so objective as if it were about a foreign nation. That is America's strength. May she never lose it. The worst corruptions always come from weakness. But soon America will want her citizens to be a little more Prussian.

The violent rebellion that erupted in the African-American district of Los Angeles that same month contributed to my radicalization—or at least made me more aware of how radical my attitude had become. The effort to precisely articulate my views made me conscious of harboring a hostility that, in its intensity, came as a surprise, a revelation, even to me. Some would certainly describe this hostility as "anti-American," an epithet that, because it suggests an irrational *a priori* hatred, always seemed to me to be a convenient way of evading, even ignoring, criticism. But even Steffi berated me: "Why can't you be proud of your country?"

The Watts riots provoked the following emotional tirade, recorded in my journal on 17 August 1965:

> The revolt in Los Angeles: a similar feeling of excitement and regret at not being there as in Elmer Street in Cambridge, on reading of the folk song festivals in Washington Square in Greenwich Village (and the arrests that followed). It is exciting to see the American system being forced to take notice of some blots of its own making, being forced to defend itself by killing. It is exciting to see that 20,000 soldiers are needed, with bayonets

fixed. It is exciting to see that there aren't enough jails to contain all the "undesirable elements." It is exciting to see a people behaving as contemptuously as they are treated. You consider them beasts and then are outraged when they behave like beasts. It is exciting to see the disregard for human life of the good and the righteous—the police. And then Americans wonder at the "inhumanity" of the communists putting the economic principle foremost.

A lot is written about the underlying causes, the discontent; few words are wasted on the 26 Negroes who lost their lives. Caption under the N.Y. Times picture of a Negro taking a pair of shoes out of a broken shop window: "Vandal helps himself to..." Dr. Martin Luther King refuses to go to Los Angeles; he knows he has no power. He would be regarded as a tool of the whites, playing their game. He is regarded with the same contempt as those who sought reforms through parliament were regarded by communists [in the Weimar Republic].

What is the ideal solution of the "Negro problem" in American eyes? If only the Negroes were different than they, the whites! If only they didn't share the same traits as the whites: greed, ambition, avarice, aggressiveness, competitiveness. Why can't they believe in non-violence and religion and humility and abnegation and be nice and black and harmless? Why aren't they satisfied with a nice little manual job and a nice little ramble-shack apartment? Why can't they fit into the system—on the lowest rung? Why do they have to pick on such unfair means to get what they want? If they like to fight so much, why don't they go to Vietnam? But then, what can you expect from people without education. The figures on illiteracy and income are supposed to explain everything: they are the nation's contempt expressed in statistics.

The connection between Vietnam and the urban riots, both of which escalated dramatically in 1965, seemed obvious to me. When I first heard on AFN of the launching of "retaliatory" air strikes against North Vietnam in late 1964 and the full-scale intervention in 1965 I could hardly believe what I heard. It seemed almost surrealistic, like a spoof deliberately put on to demonstrate the absurdity of American policy, but falling flat and failing in its purpose—because people actually took the threat from Ho Chi Minh's nationalist movement (based on the principles of the American war of independence) seriously. In December 1965 I reflected at length on the difficulty and apparent futility of resistance to the war and the problematic relationship between morality and power:

> We may "suspect" that others are wrong; we may even offer excellent arguments for our suspicion, but we are unable to "prove" others wrong, except from a vantage point of greater power. This is the problem of any kind of "resistance": it is so hard to *prove* the American intervention in Vietnam is wrong, for instance, as long as everything goes according to plan, successes are recorded, and even the opponents seem by their actions or reactions at times to grant the validity of the American undertaking. The moral force, it seems, is simply not strong enough to win out. It is not that one lacks the courage to pit oneself against superior power. It is simply that one is not sure enough of oneself to overcome the tremendous right(eous)ness on all sides, and the power of mere numbers can't be denied. When everyone around one is "right," and events even confirm this rightness instead of putting it into question, it is very difficult to appear anything but ridiculous, anything but a Don Qixote, to run up against them.
>
> It is this that must account for the minimal effective resistance to Hitler within Germany before and during the Second World War. But this does not mean that moral force does not in the end decide the battle. Precisely in the case of Vietnam one is enormously aware of the importance of moral force: one realizes instinctively that America will only then be beaten when its soldiers begin to question their cause. (This awareness is quite unlike my hazy childhood conception—especially in thinking about Mama's statement that Germany had lost the war because they had been in the wrong—that being right somehow had a magic power of its own.) No wonder that *Die Welt*, in an enraging and frustrating editorial, criticizes the American government for allowing a dissident minority to undermine its confidence that its Vietnam policy is right. No wonder that defeatism was a capital crime in Nazi Germany.

In January 1966 I reacted to Johnson's State of the Union speech:

> "...To work for peace , and all the wonderful , marvelous fruits of peace." A good definition of war.

> "The state of the union is such as to allow us both to fight in Vietnam and to realize the objectives of the Great Society at the same time." Ah, paradise on earth.
>
> "We will strive to limit the conflict ..." Now, no one will get hurt, if you just do as we say...

In October 1966, after my argument with Olaf, I again resorted to sarcasm in my journal under the heading "Attempt at a propagandistic statement of my views on Vietnam":

> "We are ready to end the war here and now..." says Johnson. How magnificently generous to offer to stop bombing other people's homes, bridges, roads, and railways! "...if the North Vietnamese will stop their aggression against South Vietnam."
>
> This is a case of the "West" being technically, legally, in the right, the "East," however, being right in principle.
>
> If the U. S. really had the welfare of the Vietnamese at heart, they would allow the unification of Vietnam under a nationalist-communist regime, instead of turning it into a battleground.
>
> There is aggression, "invasion," on both sides. Which is the greater aggression? The North Vietnamese support for a civil uprising in the South against a government presently headed by a (renegade) North Vietnamese, General Ky, or the American invasion over a distance of thousands of miles to crush a rebellion against a military dictatorship?
>
> The whole nature of American life is aggressive: for ideological domination (if for the moment we grant that the tyranny of "freedom" is not as restrictive as communism) it substitutes economic dominance.
>
> For Americans the war is a crusade; for the Vietnamese it is the very purpose of life: against, and only against America can this identification of national purpose be achieved.

Nonetheless, as we now know, resistance to the war grew among Americans and even reached Berlin, where a former army officer founded an organization called "U.S. Campaign" to persuade Americans abroad to oppose the war. In my journal I recorded my meeting with him in the lobby of the *Hartnackschule* in April 1967, where he tried to enlist me in the anti-war cause:

> Meeting Mr Fuller of the "U.S. Campaign" yesterday. He assured me that he was not a "peacenik," a dissenter for the sake of dissent. "My father is a colonel, I'm a Republican. I'm not a draft-dodger or anything like that. We feel this war is not good for the country. It's too expensive for one thing. I'm going around talking to people. I've talked to thousands of people in this city, telling them our views."
>
> Why did I feel so uncomfortable? Only because I'm so unused to speaking English? Or to be taken for what I wasn't (I would undoubtedly have felt more comfortable if they had been preaching revolution instead of "encouraging a political settlement")? Or because he was a captain in the army? This is the voice I must continually stifle: I don't just want to change your "policy" on Vietnam. I want to change your values!

I *was* the "peacenik" with whom Mr. Fuller refused to identify. But I was delighted to learn from this encounter that evidently I was not the only one "just sitting in Berlin and criticizing!" Fuller and his fellow members of the U.S Campaign were not content to just criticize, however; unlike me they were actively engaged in the cause of peace.

There was another reason for my hesitation to openly join Fuller's peace campaign. It had to do with my dual citizenship, and the bad conscience it aroused. Through Papa I had obtained a German passport and identity card back in 1960. I made use of my German citizenship simply because it made it much easier to obtain employment, cheap housing, health insurance, and, if I stayed in Germany, an old-age pension. It certainly eliminated a lot of red tape. But I had no intention of giving up my American citizenship or risking its loss. In March 1965, when renewing my passport at the U.S. consulate, I worried about committing "my first consciously illegal act—swearing never to have 'sought or claimed the benefits of nationality of any foreign states'." In those days the U. S. did not permit dual citizenship; making use of the citizenship of another nation was viewed as tantamount to renouncing U.S. citizenship. All this has changed today as a consequence of several lawsuits brought in the late 1960s. Today, for instance, Americans can even join the Israeli Defense Forces without losing their American citizenship. Proscription of making use of the privileges of foreign citizenship was in any case very difficult for State Department officials to monitor and enforce. But in 1965 it was still a source of worry to me. Although I was not yet certain about my future plans—they would be decided in consultation with Steffi—I did not want to close off the option of returning home. I remembered Mama's warning about expatriation: "It catches up on you in middle age." She had been very concerned that Tempy, who spent five years in Germany from 1958 to 1963, might decide to stay: "He doesn't belong there." Steffi's reaction to my passport troubles was refreshingly unflappable: *"Du bist viel menschlicher wenn du Sorgen hast"* (you're much more human when you have worries). My older Lithuanian friend Pavel Navacelskis, who had been brought to Germany as a forced laborer during the war and had never returned home, sought to console me: "The whole world is in a mess."

My citizenship muddle and emotional attachment to Germany inevitably gave rise to self-questioning, as recorded in outline form in my journal on 15 March 1965:

> At odd moments I catch a glimpse of my personality as peculiarly identical with Germany, particularly its weaknesses: seriousness to the point of gravity and solemnity; desperately wanting to do things right; hyper-sensitive to the reactions of others; tendency to intolerance and even contempt toward those unlike us; tendency to confession and self-justification and self-analysis (as at present); secret conviction (careful not to show it, though) of being superior and important; a certain lethargy or indolence in attitude toward novelty and change; easily thrown out of equilibrium if things aren't just so; this sentimental sincerity; the psychological need of a justification (usually personal gain of some sort) for everything one does; a certain heaviness (inertia) which is at once a shackle (a lead-footedness) and a force (when set in motion); the need for security and order and method, a settled little paradise; the suicidal, the sacrificial, the hysterical, the stubborn, the miserly or the profligate, but nothing in-between. Germany's egoism, her "go-it-alone-ism," her fight against (and courtship of) the "others." Choosing Germany simply to identify myself with the unpopular; psychologically suited to Germany as the "defeated," free of the responsibilities of power; my neuroses not so noticeable in Germany.

Once in this half playful, half-serious mood of free association, I began to see my parents and siblings in terms of national characteristics and rivalries as well. Olaf was France, the home of intellect, enlightenment, rationality, and moderation; Betsy was Italy, beautiful vacation land but temperamental and fickle, attracted to power and art, but too quick to change sides; Tempy was England, witty, self-controlled, active, resilient, with a tendency to strut and often beset by economic difficulties due to excessively ambitious expenditures; Papa was Russia, huge in every way, including the capacity to work and to celebrate, to eat and to drink, a vast capacity for socializing, accompanied by a susceptibility to socialization and conformity, full of feeling and ideals, but with a sense of fairness, authority, and order—and (at the time at least) surrounded by satellites; Mama was, of course, America, the source of enormous moral strength, lean and tough, undefeated and undefeatable, with her own satellites—tougher ones on the whole than Russia's satellites, because more independent. I identified with post-war West Germany,

> aware of my past sins (though unable to completely eradicate them), proud of my present self-examination, embarrassed at my previous behavior, though at times nostalgic for my previous power, feeling my identity and virtue by opposing Russia (for whom I have considerable admiration), gaining my strength from my Americanization, living for a nod of approval from America, eager to integrate with my European siblings.

Our decision to go (back) to America was made after the birth of our daughter Trina in April 1966. This thrilling event made me aware not only of my obligation to secure her future, but also quite uneasy about the low opinion I might eventually merit in her eyes if I did not attain a higher level of achievement than my accomplishments to date. Pressures to succeed and prosper are generally thought to emanate from parents, but in my case the wish to live up to what I thought would be the new arrival's hopes and expectations generated the greatest motive force of all. My return to America was only a question of timing for me; Steffi, on the other hand, had to be persuaded to so abruptly leave her native land. I convinced her I could get a better-paying job in the U. S., an important consideration now that there would be at least three mouths to feed.

We had married on 10 October 1965 in a civil ceremony, with only our two witnesses present, my theologian friend Olaf and his wife Karin, whom we then invited to a lunch at home. Ulrike, writing a congratulatory card to her sister from Paris, could not resist the good-natured gibe, "*Wie ist es nun mit dem genialen Leben?*"—a reference to Steffi's previously-expressed disdain for the bourgeois institutions of marriage and motherhood. At least no one could accuse us of celebrating our wedding in the conventional bourgeois way. As previously agreed, should the date of the civil ceremony fall on the day my chess club met—a quite likely eventuality because of the crowded schedule at the *Standesamt* and our relative impatience to get the formalities behind us—I would attend the chess club meeting that evening. In retrospect, this was, of course, a major mistake. Not only was I wrong to think Steffi had meant it when she said she didn't mind, but her family strongly disapproved of what seemed like a callous act, and even my friends reacted with disbelief that I would play chess on the evening of my wedding day.

My brother Olaf happened to be in Berlin for a conference of Humboldt fellows on the day that Trini was born, 26 April 1966. We named her Katherine Ellen, prompting Mama to write, "I was quite thrilled to hear that Ellen was among her names!" Her birth occurred a few days before her official due date, as I recall. Unexpectedly, Steffi's water burst while on an after-supper stroll—possibly because she had spent the previous day whitewashing her entire *Werkstatt*, an obvious example of preparing the nest. I was much more nervous than Steffi herself, leaving Olaf to accompany Steffi home as I raced to fetch a taxi. The baby was born several hours after her admission to the maternity ward. As it was late, and the birth was not expected before morning, I was told to go home, where I would be informed of the birth by phone. In those days fathers were not allowed, much less expected, to be present at the birth of their child. I spent a restless night, feeling nauseous at the thought of the pain I had inflicted on Steffi and vowing never to put her through such an ordeal again. When I got the news of my daughter's birth in the morning, I was enveloped by waves of affection for the baby for coming to join us in our Möckernstrasse abode and sharing our unconventional and penurious life—all, as it seemed, on her own volition. Both Steffi and I had expected a boy, not necessarily because of any strong personal preference, but only because Steffi, with her "masculine" drive and assertiveness, seemed to be a natural breeder of boys. It never occurred to us that my own "feminine" traits of frailty and passivity might throw into doubt our androcentric expectations! In my journal I recorded the following "Thoughts on it being a girl," reflecting the rather sexist assumptions of an era preceding the just emerging powerful second wave of the feminist movement, soon to be known as the Women's Liberation Movement:

> It seems less of a challenge or threat than a son; I am not so afraid of its opinion. It is more relaxing. But it ties me up more with the world. It is less independent. It will be less able to make its own way. A girl is more to be loved, a son more to be proud of.

Needless to say, all these fears and worries turned out to be entirely groundless, as Trina went on to a successful career that included a doctorate from the Harvard School of Public Health in 2006. Yet when Steffi's friend and fellow-goldsmith Bärbel Reister gave birth to a son a year after Trina's birth, Steffi asked me, to my considerable annoyance, whether I was envious. I felt she might have asked me that question to conceal or combat potential feelings of envy in herself.

We were typically nervous parents, once even taking our *Butzele* to the hospital because her stool had a slightly greenish tinge, a perfectly normal result of a milk diet. Steffi boiled the diapers daily on the two-burner hotplate that served as our stove, prompting Karin Meyer to say, "I wouldn't want to have a baby without a washing mashine." Yet we didn't even have a bathtub or a shower!

As a concession to Steffi's mother, we had the child baptized in the Lutheran faith of her family.

> The *Pfarrer* (pastor), whom Steffi had described as "Prussian" and whom I therefore had expected to be distant and stuffy, proved to be rather too familiar. He made the impression of someone who has had practice ingratiating himself with tough guys—like a prison parson or military chaplain—only in his case the heathens he had to cope with were primarily businessmen, judging by the anecdotes he told in his sermon: "In a conversation with a *Kaufmann* (merchant) I recently said, 'If you charge a profit margin of 50 percent, you are no Christian.' He replied, "But *Herr Pfarrer,* what does *Christlichkeit* (being a Christian) have to do with my business?' And I said, 'Everything!' Yes, my dear brothers and sisters, we are all a little schizophrenic, you see. We all have a split consciousness. *Jawohl.* We actually make a separation between *Christlichkeit* and life. We think we are Christian because we go to church

on Sundays, and we think we can then forget everything during the week. We are all, more or less, *Sonntagschristen*, my dear brothers and sisters. And, you see, that is not genuine *Christlichkeit*..." And so on.

"Fashion comes and goes. It changes every few years. The Church does not need to follow the fashion. We are strong enough to endure." At times he seemed to be advertising the benefits of belonging to his club, at other times he seemed to be threatening those that didn't.

In this noisy power talk with all its rhetorical and histrionic flourishes, the cry of the baby seemed to be the only human sound.

He had the assistance of nature at one point: the sun began to shine into the church just as he was saying, "And the Lord Jesus Christ is coming to us." He had the wisdom not to draw attention to it, though. I was irritated at his luck, and yet pleased, because I knew Tante Tatjana was enjoying it so much. Tante Lilla thought he was good, too, although she had been alienated somewhat at first to have been called schizophrenic. *"Na, weisst du!"* Only Ulrike, whose instincts I have noticed to be quite sound on a number of other occasions, but always, when asked, for the wrong reasons, thought the *Pfarrer* was terrible. *"So ein blödes Geschwätz* (such idiotic prattle). One really can`t take it seriously. And then constantly this 'my dear brothers and sisters.'"

In the summer of 1966 I began writing application letters to American secondary schools. Teaching offered the best potential for an interesting job with a reasonable income. Secondary school teaching was the only level for which I was qualified, and I knew I was good at it. When I began receiving affirmative replies in the fall, we made our definitive decision to leave for America by the late spring or early summer of 1967, as soon after the expiration of our Möckernstrasse lease as we could arrange. I did have to wrestle with a tempting option to stay in Berlin. When Lauterbach heard of my plans to leave, he made a quite unexpected and flattering offer. As he had no children, and his wife was now in her mid-forties, he offered to make me a partner in the *Hartnackschule* and thus effectively his heir. The details were a bit vague, however, especially in regard to how this "promotion" would affect my immediate duties and income and what my role in management and decision-making would be up to his retirement or death. Moreover, the relatively youthful Frau Lauterbach was even more active than her aging husband in running the school, especially in her role as treasurer. I realized it would probably be thirty years or more before she would want to relinquish control. Nonetheless, we did briefly consider staying in Berlin, and even looked at apartments, but found that it would be very difficult to find a place that offered the flexibility of the Möckernstrasse dwelling at a reasonable price. Years later, after the fall of the Berlin wall, when I revisited the Hartnackschule, I found it had expanded into a new and roomier building to accommodate its ever-growing number of students, now mostly immigrants learning German. I could not help but wonder whether I had not made a mistake to turn down the Lauterbachs` offer those many years before.

Mama did her part to facilitate our return to America by offering to let us stay in a two-room hut she had built on her land, at least until we found a place of our own. She also spoke to the superintendent of schools for this part of northern Vermont, Mr. Pelkey, who was looking for faculty to staff a new regional high school scheduled to open in the fall of 1967. Pelkey, who was taking a study tour of Scandinavia for school administrators, invited me to an interview in Copenhagen in April 1967. I did not know at the time that he was an alcoholic, but felt very much relieved of my nervousness by his question, when we got together for our 2 p.m. interview, whether I′d like to join him in a Schnaps. I was delighted to do so, which made a very favorable impression on him. However, he had probably already made up his mind to hire me even before the interview, as five minutes into the interview he pulled out a completed contract for me to sign. In those heady days of increasing federal funding of education amid a booming war economy, rural schools in particular faced a shortage of teachers in many parts of the country. Jobs were not hard to get. However, I was somewhat embarrassed to learn that on my job application I had spelled "address" in the German way with one "d," not a good sign for someone applying for a job to teach English. "Think nothing of it," Pelkey said, "I′m a bad speller myself."

My last days at the *Hartnackschule* were wonderfully brightened by thoughts of our impending departure and the adventures that lay ahead. The only class I would really miss was a lively advanced German-language class with about 30 foreign students from all over the world. They knew enough German to make thoughtful conversations and even classroom debates quite feasible, and many of them could also speak or at least understand English. It was not difficult to find topics on which everyone seemed to have an opinion. One such issue was the Israeli-Palestinian conflict, which was hotly debated in class. The half-dozen or so students from Arab countries vigorously defended Palestinian interests, but found themselves in a minority. One student from Syria, in particular, hurt his cause by his boastful exaggeration of the Arab side's military superiority. A far larger number of students, especially those from European countries, sided with Israel in the Six-Day War in early June 1967, reflecting also the dominant public opinion in Berlin and in Germany at the time. The unexpectedly decisive Israeli victory left the Syrian student embarrassed and chastened and open to the derision of many of his fellow students. However, I felt more sorry for the only Palestinian in my class, whose family owned a hotel in East Jerusalem. I told him not to worry; the Israelis would respect their property rights. Events, of course, would prove me entirely wrong.

Epilogue

I returned to America in June 1967, a failure by any normal criteria of vocational or professional success. It marked a new beginning, but not yet, as it turned out, the end of my *Wanderjahre*, nor, for that matter, of my long journey "out from Hitler's shadow." After two years of teaching high-school English and social studies in northern Vermont, I returned to graduate school in history at the University of Vermont and the University of Massachusetts at Amherst, finally earning my PhD with a specialization in modern Germany and intellectual history in 1974. The very tight job market took me to temporary positions at San Diego State University, the University of Oregon, and the University of South Dakota, before I gratefully accepted a tenure-track offer at Gonzaga University in Spokane, Washington. These peregrinations will be covered in a subsequent volume.

My efforts to explore and come to terms with my past had only begun. My career as a historian of Germany in the American provinces was to take me much deeper into that quest. Although I might not have acknowledged it at the time, the first part of my life served as a much better preparation for this voyage of discovery than I might have expected. However, the fruits of these early experiences were not to be harvested for many more years.